LOADED

loaded

money
and the
spirituality
of
enough

Heather King

Franciscan
MEDIA
Cincinnati, Ohio

Cover design by Kathleen Lynch | Black Kat Design
Book design by Mark Sullivan
Cover image © istock | alynst

LIBRARY OF CONGRESS CATALOGING-IN-PUBLICATION DATA
Names: King, Heather, 1952– author.
Title: Loaded : money and the spirituality of enough / Heather King.
Description: Cincinnati : Franciscan Media, 2016.
Identifiers: LCCN 2016002485 | ISBN 9781616369590 (pbk.)
Subjects: LCSH: Money. | Wealth. | Money—Religious aspects.
Classification: LCC HG221 .K496 2016 | DDC 241/.68—dc23
LC record available at http://lccn.loc.gov/2016002485

Published by Franciscan Media
28 W. Liberty St.
Cincinnati, OH 45202
www.FranciscanMedia.org

Printed in the United States of America.
Printed on acid-free paper.
16 17 18 19 20 5 4 3 2 1

For my sister Jeanne
and for her Jimmy

load·ed

adj.

1. Carrying a load.

2. Equipped with many accessories or features.

3. Heavy with meaning or emotional import: The psychoanalyst special-ized in asking loaded questions.

4. Slang: Drunk or intoxicated.

5. Slang: Having a great deal of money. See synonyms at "rich."

Do not store up for yourselves treasures on earth, where moth and decay destroy, and thieves break in and steal. But store up treasures in heaven, where neither moth nor decay destroys, nor thieves break in and steal. For where your treasure is, there also will your heart be.

—Matthew 6:19–21

CONTENTS

CONTENTS

THE GOSPEL CALL AND OUR MONEY WOUNDS

In 1987, I got sober. In 1990, with the law degree I'd earned while drinking, I landed a job as an attorney and started making money for the first time I my life. In 1994, I quit that job in order to embark on the precarious vocation of a writer. In 1996, I converted to Catholicism and joined the Church.

To quit that job as a lawyer was one of the biggest leaps into the unknown, requiring the most heart, of my life.

I gave up making $72,000 a year with benefits.

I made almost no money from creative writing for the first ten years. I supported myself with a part-time job writing legal motions and briefs. I have never for one second wavered from the knowledge that my decision was right, nor have I for one second regretted it.

Since then, I have, however, become increasingly fascinated by the "economy" described in the Gospels—the parable of the prodigal son (Luke 15:11–32); the worker who comes late to the vineyard and receives the same pay as those who came early (Matthew 20:1–16); the familiar "No one can serve two masters. He will either hate one, and love the other; or be devoted to one, and despise the other. You cannot serve God and mammon" (Matthew 6:24).

In fact, Christ had reams to say about money, earning, vocation. "It is harder for a rich man to enter the kingdom of heaven than for a camel to pass through the eye of a needle." "Don't worry about what you are to eat and what you are to wear, your Heavenly Father knows what you need before you ask him." "Regard the lilies of the field." "Blessed are the poor." "Give the hungry some of your bread and the naked some of your clothing." "Take with you no purse or bag or sandals." "If a man asks for your tunic, give him your cloak also."

THE GOSPEL CALL TO VOLUNTARY POVERTY

While the Church allows for ownership of private property, in a doctrine called "The Universal Destination and the Private Ownership of Goods" she also makes clear that the goods of creation are for the whole human race.

Paragraph 2402 from the *Catechism of the Catholic Church:*

> In the beginning God entrusted the earth and its resources to the common stewardship of mankind to take care of them, master them by labor, and enjoy their fruits. The goods of creation are destined for the whole human race. However, the earth is divided up among men to assure the security of their lives, endangered by poverty and threatened by violence. The appropriation of property is legitimate for guaranteeing the freedom and dignity of persons and for helping each of them to meet his basic needs and the needs of those in his charge. It should allow for a natural solidarity to develop between men.

Paragraph 2403 from the *Catechism of the Catholic Church:*

> The right to private property, acquired or received in a just way, does not do away with the original gift of the earth to the whole of mankind. The universal destination of goods remains primordial, even if the promotion of the common good requires respect for the right to private property and its exercise.

During his public life, Christ himself seems to have owned few to no private goods and also to have been entirely unconcerned with money. He seems to have carried no money on his person. When he needed a coin for the temple tax, he told Peter to go catch a fish and open its mouth and there he would find a coin. That Judas, the one who would betray him, was also the one who kept the purse was probably no accident. Christ didn't despise money; he just didn't think about money, or at least he didn't worry about money. He seemed to live in supreme confidence that money would come if and when it was needed.

But Christ had lived for thirty years prior to that. He came from a family that was poor and marginalized. He worked with his hands, presumably beside his father, as a carpenter. He didn't pull the parable of the workers in the vineyard, the parable of the unjust steward, or the parable of the talents out of thin air. He'd worked for rich people who had stiffed him, for wealthy merchants who drove a hard bargain, for homeowners who tried to wring out of him every last shekel and never offered him so much as a glass of water while he toiled in the hot sun. Like us, he had to negotiate contracts, prices, working hours, benefits. Like us, he worked at times, out of necessity, for liars, profiteers, and cheats.

Like us, he lived in a time when people tried to make God into a product, a package, a marketing opportunity.

He drove the money-changers out of the temple with a whip.

He knew human nature well.

But like his mother, he also pondered these things in his heart. He knew there will always be money-changers in the temple but he also knew that in the Gospel economy, nothing from love is ever wasted: not one lost coin, not a single wandering sheep, not one hair from our heads.

He lifted sore-covered Lazarus from his station by the gate to heaven, while the rich man suffered the torments of hell. He praised the Good Samaritan who bound up the wounds of a stranger and bought him a room for the night. He loved the one who gave much because she had been forgiven much. He marveled at the generosity of spirit in the widow who gave her last two mites.

Clearly, to live with little more than we need is part of the basic Gospel call.

Clearly, in a culture sickened by materialism, gluttony and greed of all kinds, our call to live simply and to share abundantly is more pressing than ever.

Perhaps you are nodding in agreement, for there are many of us for whom voluntary poverty is a very real ideal.

But just as clearly, many of us are also in various kinds of bondage around money.

We overspend. We all know what that means, and how that goes.

We underearn—and by that I mean, we confuse voluntary poverty with a nearly pathological self-deprivation. We think God isn't interested in anything as mundane as our "money lives."

We can live in terrible fear around money. We can equate poverty in and of itself with holiness. We can live in neurotic guilt that we have *any* money at all. We can secretly think we're not good enough to deserve money or to do what we're passionate about for work. Poverty can become an idol just as much as wealth.

That's when things can get compulsive.

I should know.

OUR MONEY WOUNDS

Many, if not most, people who make the decision to live in voluntary poverty do so from a house built on solid spiritual rock and from sound mental health. My decision to give up the money and switch from lawyering to writing was one of the most life-enhancing, healthy, sane, loving choices of my life. But, like many others, I had wounds around money, and unbeknownst to me at the time, I brought them all with me.

Examining these wounds is of the utmost importance because, unhealed, the wounds block us from God: from all that is free, true, beautiful, creative, and good. In the parable of the paralytic lowered down from the roof by his friends (Luke 5:17–26) Christ says, in effect, "What's a bigger miracle, a physical healing or the psycho-spiritual healing that comes from being forgiven for and delivered from our sins?" If you've been delivered from an obsessive-compulsive addiction like alcoholism, as I have, you know that the spiritual healing is by far the more miraculous. To have the power to deliver a human being from the bondage of alcohol is infinitely more remarkable than being able to command a mountain to move and having the mountain move.

Recognizing the ways we need to be healed, and then being open to being healed, requires tremendous self-honesty, tremendous vulnerability, tremendous humility, and a tremendous capacity to stretch way, way beyond our comfort zones.

That is precisely the Gospel journey. In *Breathing Underwater: Spirituality and the Twelve Steps*, Franciscan Richard Rohr writes:

> It is my experience after over forty years as a priest that we could say…about many well-intentioned Christians and clergy…[that] [t]heir religion has never touched them or healed them at the unconscious level where all of the real motivation, hurts, unforgiveness, anger, wounds, and illusions are stored, hiding—and often fully operative. They never went to "the inner room" where Jesus invited us, and where things hid "secretly" (Matthew 6:6).[1]

Later, he observes:

> People only come to deeper consciousness *by intentional struggles with contradictions, conflicts, inconsistencies, inner confusions,* and what the biblical tradition calls "sin" or moral failure. Starting with Adam and Eve, there seems to be a necessary "transgression" that sets the whole human story into motion. In Paul's brilliant exposé on the spiritual function of law, his letter to the Romans, he actually says that "the law was given to multiply the opportunities of falling!" Now deal with that one. And then he adds, "so that grace can even be greater" (5:20–21)! *God actually relishes the*

vacuum, which God knows, God alone can fill. St. Thérèse of Lisieux called this her "little way," which is nothing other than the Gospel itself. "Whoever is a little one, let him come to me" (Proverbs 9:4) became her mantra and her message.[2]

Our wounds in any one area of our lives bleed over into every other area.

Christ helped the deaf to hear, the blind to see, the lame to walk, and the paralytic to get up off his mat. But all those people wanted, desperately, to be healed. Christ can only heal us when we've acknowledged how very blind we are, how very deaf, how very paralyzed.

Again, the Gospel journey is precisely about cultivating the desire, the humility, the courage, and the love to uncover these unconscious wounds and self-defeating patterns that can dictate the course of our lives. We get to take a look at our resentments, our fears, the people to whom we owe amends. We get to invite God into every area of our lives—especially the parts that are most conflicted, most wounded.

THREE WAYS THE WOUND CAN MANIFEST

So examining our wounds is essential to wholeness in our lives. In my experience, wounds around money can become forms of *involuntary* poverty: poverty of imagination, poverty of faith. Here are three main ways that I have seen it happen.

—Staying in a low-paying job we don't like because we're too afraid to apply for something more challenging, go to school to get a degree, or otherwise intellectually, emotionally, and spiritually stretch.

—Staying in a high-paying job we don't like out of fear of giving up the benefits or pay.

—Staying stuck in a job, no matter what the pay, because we don't know what we really want to do; or because though we do know, we tell ourselves that to follow our hearts is somehow impossible.

At different times of my life, I've suffered from and gone a long way toward working through all three of these.

So, as you've now assuredly figured out, unlike so many money books, mine is not about how to make more and consume more. It's about how to detach from the idea that our identity could possibly lie in how much or how little money we make or have. It's about discovering that money is a means of love and service. It's about learning that the real economy is "As you give, so shall you receive." We get to follow the deepest desires of our heart. The money will come. *And we'll want to share it.*

That hasn't happened for me by praying a whole bunch of rosaries, holing up in my room, and hoping for the best. The solution for me and many people I know has involved clarity around numbers—how much we spend, how much we earn. It has been clarity around how we spend our time. And it's been community—meaning friends, a realistic acceptance of the fact that we're not going to change overnight, and laughs.

To that end, *Loaded* is divided into seven sections: The Truth: The Law of Love; The Lie: The Law of Fear; Coming Awake; Forensics; Healing; Dating Our Dreams; and Leap. The approach is proactive, structured around a series of simple yet transformative actions. Tools, jokes, and practical tips abound. I'll chart my own recovery around money and several others will tell their stories, too. The language will be familiar to those in recovery for addictions of various kinds, and easily accessible to those who aren't.

Wherever you fall on the spectrum between freedom and bondage around money, I believe that these stories and tools will help. And the underlying principles—clarity, honesty, the confluence of will and grace—apply in every area of our lives.

PART ONE

THE TRUTH

The Law of Love

CHAPTER ONE

TWO CATHOLIC WORKERS TELL THEIR STORY

Loaded is about earning, spending, and serving in love. Above all, the purpose of this book is to explore how we might spend as much of our time as possible doing what we love.

To that end, I want to start with the story of two dear friends of mine. Tensie Hernandez and Dennis Apel were married eighteen years ago and have two kids: Rozella, sixteen, and Thomas, fourteen.

As founders and community members of the Guadalupe (California) Catholic Worker, they distribute food and clothing to the poor, run a small free clinic, and regularly vigil at Vandenberg Air Force Base. They live by the Gospel, in other words. And they are two of the freest people around money I know.

DENNIS: We Live with Some Precarity
Dennis, sixty-four, grew up in Downey, California.

"I'm a cradle Catholic. I wanted to become a priest and, after high school, entered a Franciscan seminary. The idea of service and voluntary poverty and being with the outcast had always attracted me deeply.

"After a year I left. My parish priest hooked me up with a man who was dying. I began to visit Gerald regularly. I talked to him. He could nod his head, he could squeeze my hand. He died, but he had someone to come to see him, and I felt good about that.

"I did more work with the sick and the dying. By this time, I was married with two kids. I went to 6:30 Mass every morning for four years. I was praying. Hard. The real thing. Because I was working as a salesman for a trucking company but that's not what I was supposed to do or liked to do. I knew that and I decided that if God was ever going to get me out of sales, I had some work to do. So I started paying down my debts, because I was going to theaters and restaurants and ball games and I went hunting and golfing and I was given a new car every three years and I could charge things up on credit cards. I had a house.

"I started paying all those things off. I wanted to get debt-free. About the time I did get debt-free, I got a call from Fr. Don Cribs who was head chaplain at County USC Hospital in LA. He asked, 'Would you like to quit sales and come work for me?' I said, 'Sure.'

"He said, 'Tell me what you need.' I was making $80,000 a year, health insurance, an unlimited expense account. I went home and figured out our finances, and I went back and told Fr. Don I think it was $29,000 and he agreed. So I gave two weeks' notice at a place I'd been at eleven and a half years and went to work for this priest at USC County Hospital, the dumping ground for the uninsured of LA.

"My wife was terribly unhappy. I was thirty-seven, thirty-eight by this time.

"Post-surgery patients at the hospital would have no place to go. They were street people. So when they were about to be discharged, we'd call the LA Catholic Worker (whose house is close to County Hospital), and ask if the patient could stay a couple of weeks, and they'd say, 'Sure, bring him over.'

"That's how I met Tensie. She was living at the Catholic Worker house at the time. I'd bring patients over and she'd receive them. She was so beautiful, both physically and in her spirit.

"At the same time, all this stuff was going on in El Salvador and we had what we called the Wednesday morning coalition. Me and other activists from LA—priests, laypeople, a group of a hundred or so— would march to the Federal Building in downtown LA and surround it, sometimes chain ourselves to the door, and get arrested. I'd see Tensie there, because the LA Catholic Worker was involved.

"It was my first introduction to the application of the Gospel to something besides myself. The first understanding that as a collective group, we're complicit in people's sufferings because of the decisions that our government's making with our approval, our blessing almost, that are so contrary to the teachings of Christ.

"I was being re-formed. And working at County Hospital, I was seeing the poor, the poor, the poor. You see what Tensie and I call the 'Beatitudes People.' People whose lives have been really, really tough. They're in predicaments. You see they've received the burden of unhealed wounds—poverty, addiction—that have been passed down for generations.

"I had my feet in two worlds, a very uncomfortable place to be. At home my wife was wanting to maintain the lifestyle we'd had for years. And I was not only unable to do that, I didn't want to do that anymore. So the marriage was going, going, going. And it was very painful.

"Finally, I got a divorce. Soon after, Tensie and I got together. We decided to move to Northern California and joined the Oakland Catholic Worker. We turned out not to be a good fit for the community. But where to go from here? We'd walk for hours, up and down the Berkeley Pier, saying *What are we gonna do, what are we gonna do?* We got a notebook and on one page we wrote 'What We Know We Want' and on another page we wrote, 'What We Know We Don't Want.' That's the best we could come up with.

"We didn't want to be big city any more. We didn't want to be Catholic Workers anymore. We didn't want to live on donations anymore. We wanted to support ourselves.

"We started driving up and down the coast exploring, looking for somewhere to live and to serve. We thought we'd like to be around people who were struggling, probably Spanish-speaking people since we both spoke Spanish. We wanted to be where there was beauty all around. When we left Oakland, we had two hundred dollars, an old Volkswagen bus, our clothes, and some bicycles. We had our list, and we decided on

Guadalupe, a small, geographically isolated town on the ocean. Lots of farm workers.

"A friend offered to let us stay at her place in an adjacent town until we got on our feet. Which was lovely. We'd ride our bikes down every day to Guadalupe, look for an apartment, look for a job, neither of which we found. But we did come across a big old white Victorian-style house that was empty. It was all overgrown. We went to City Hall, discovered who the owner was, called. She said, 'Nah, I rented that house for a long time and I had nothing but problems. But I'll come out to talk to you anyway. Why don't you meet me out at the house at five on Friday?'

"We liked the house, but it was too big for us. Plus, how would we pay rent? We had no jobs!

"The day we were supposed to meet the owners we parked a block away, because the van was so ratty we didn't want them to see it. We stood down the street and watched them drive up. We kept saying, 'They won't like us, let's just not show up, let's just not show up.'

"But on the back of their car was a bumper sticker saying *Uvas, no*. 'No Grapes.' We said, 'Look at that, a United Farm Workers sticker.' So we went down and met with the couple. They took us all through the house, they got all done and they said, 'Well, we have an appointment and we have to go but we thought we'd get a bite to eat here in Guadalupe. Can we buy you dinner?' So we said, 'Well, sure, OK.' The place didn't serve alcohol, but the husband wanted beer with his Mexican food so he said, 'If I go get a six-pack, will you have a beer with me?' I said, 'Sure.'

So we sat there and it turned out we had a mutual friend. Fr. Chris Ponnet, who'd been appointed the new head of the chaplaincy training program at County Hospital just before I left, and had also recently performed the marriage of their daughter. So we had an instant connection with these people. And we told them right away that we had neither money nor jobs.

"It was a Friday and they said, 'Well let's all think about it over the weekend.' So we called the LA Worker and we said, 'You're not going to believe it but we found this house in Guadalupe and it'd make kind of a great place.' We hadn't wanted to go the Worker route but somehow things were falling into place. So they said, 'We're having a meeting this afternoon, let us get back to you.' So they got back to us and they said, 'As a community we decided we'd like to send you 500 bucks a month.' Well, that's something! Then, the owners called us back on Monday and said, 'We've thought about it and we'd really like to rent the house to you and we'd like to cut the rent way down because of what you want to do with it—could you afford 450 a month?'

"Yes! That even left us fifty bucks a month for food. We'd come two weeks earlier with 200 bucks. We were really pinching it. So that felt great.

"June 1, 1996, we moved in. We had a blow-up air mattress that didn't hold air, a little hibachi we cooked on, and a cooler to keep food in. That's all we had in the way of household goods.

"By July 1, a month later, we had a stove, a refrigerator, a dinette set, furniture for the entire living room, beds for all four upstairs bedrooms. A stove and refrigerator, a washer and dryer. A nun at the local hospital gave us eight place settings from the hospital cafeteria.

"Theologian Ched Myers calls that 'Sabbath economics.' It sounds like a real nice theory, but when those economics play out in your life, it's almost startling. That's happened more than once for us. You have to trust that it's going to happen because if you try to force things, that messes it all up. And you have to be willing for it not to happen. You have to be willing to say, 'OK, well I guess that wasn't God's will.'

"A month later we had our first hospitality guest: a guy from El Salvador came to live in the house. We were doing a food distribution program, which we still run every Tuesday. We started teaching English classes. People started dropping off their used clothes and we'd make them available to whoever needs them. We're still doing that, too."

[Dennis also vigils regularly at Vandenburg Air Force Base, is regularly arrested, and has served various stints of prison time.]

"We're a long ways from voluntary poverty but we do live with some precariousness.

"Eventually we started the free health clinic. We have four doctors right now who volunteer their time.

"Tensie has a natural way with sick people. People truly experience God's love through her. Almost immediately there's a deep, deep love and connection."

But I'll let her tell it.

TENSIE: *The Spirituality of Enough*

Tensie was also born and raised in Southern California.

"I grew up with things always being really tight. My father died of a heart attack when I was ten, so my mother was a single mom. Five kids. There wasn't a whole lot of extra fluff. When the fluff came, it was really special. The yearly Easter Bob's Big Boy breakfast was big. Going to McDonald's after a doctor's appointment was big. The yearly shopping spree at K-Mart was huge. We were always very aware that we didn't have a lot of extra but neither did a lot of the people next to us so it didn't feel odd or weird. It wasn't until my oldest brother went to university at Irvine that I saw: 'Oh, so this is how the rich people live.'

"Willie always liked the finer things in life. We always teased him about it and then he went to Irvine and he finally fit in. That was my first exposure to a lot of money. Even then my perspective was from the outside.

"So my childhood set the template. I have to give credit to my mom. She always said, 'Nobody needs to have more than we have.' Growing up in a Cuban-American home, especially the Cuban side was always kind of looking down on us. They were all in Miami. But my mother would say, 'We have food, we have a home, we have a car. Nobody needs to have more than we have.' She was able to put us through school and give us a Catholic education.

"There were a couple of homes on the other block from where I lived that they called Little Tijuana. We kind of thought, *What's going on with them?* But we didn't really reach out to them as a family that I remember. Then there were the poor kids at school. I was very much aware of them and I wondered what was going on with them. But I didn't have any huge exposure to the poor until I hit LA's Skid Row when I was eighteen.

"There I encountered poverty I'd never seen—but also a wealth I'd never seen, in terms of what was offered to me at the Los Angeles Catholic Worker.

"As community members, we got room, board, and five dollars a week. That was fine with me.

"They had a friend, Uncle Pat they called him, who was an ex-United Airlines pilot. He'd take some of the LACW community members on solo flights over LA. I remember calling my mother and saying, 'You've never lived better in your life!'

"I've never thought, *I really want that pair of shoes, or this beautiful bracelet.* I've not ever been very attracted to things. If they come in, that's great. At the time, I smoked. So the five dollars went to cigarettes. That was another huge way for me to connect with guys on Skid Row, and the times I went to jail I'd smoke with the women. That was one way I had solidarity. That was very important to me.

"The first time I went to jail was when they first had street sweeps and were arresting people for having camps on the street. Jeff [Dietrich, a forty-plus-year member of the LACW] and I and a couple of others did a major action in front of one of the businesses and I got jail time. Just a week, but that was a big opening of my eyes to what jail meant. There were several women who knew me from the food line at the soup kitchen, so I was really fine. I was well cared-for: the sharing of the cigarettes, the grooming of the hair.

"I was introduced to the Catholic Worker model when I was eighteen. That's remained my model. The model is we ask for donations. We live on donations. The way I think of it is you give yourself over to the work of God, and God sustains you. I don't even like to think of it so much as voluntary poverty but more of a living in the abundance of grace and in the belief that you will be given what you need.

"Sometimes that means having to change our needs as we perceive them. But in my life, I've been taken care of again and again and again, so much so that to live any other way is not even a consideration.

"Every single thing we have needed, every single thing has come for us. I see it better now maybe than I did at the beginning. We found the house in Guadalupe, Dennis told the story, and five years later, we had Rozella. We were living there at that point, and she was born in the house.

"Even before she was born, we felt like we were in a fishbowl. There were knocks at the door constantly, people needing things, wanting help. So I put the idea of a place to live, apart from the Worker house, out there in terms of prayer. And within a couple of months, Larry (a friend of the Catholic Worker from Northern California who's connected to several wealthy donors) showed up and said, 'One of my supporters died and left a chunk of money so since you're parents now if you guys want to go find another house'....

"Right when I'd been thinking, *I don't know if we can go on like this!* Originally my thought had been a little shack, maybe in the hills. Dennis and I laugh now. I'd say, 'Honey, let's just go and see will they maybe be willing to sell that little barn behind the house that's falling down?' Dennis would say, 'Do you know how much work that is?' I'd tell him, 'It's OK, I'm sure you could do it.'

"Obviously, even a shack was so beyond what Larry was offering us. Either of us could have gotten a job, or we could have gotten a loan, to supplement the amount at hand.

"But one of our values from the beginning, and I'm really grateful, is that we never wanted to live with debt. We've never wanted to be indebted to either a paying job or a loan. First, I'd never had that experience. Second, Dennis had just finished living that kind of life. So we both said, 'We don't want that. We'll only live with whatever is given. Whatever's at hand. We don't want to incur any debt.'

"So we started looking. We didn't particularly want to come to the city of Santa Maria but we started seeing a lot of houses here. We came across this one and we thought, 'It's on a busy street. But you know what? The price is within the money that Larry had given us. So it's a castle.'

"Larry bought it outright. Then he put it in a trust. He said, 'After ten years if you continue with the work, then the house becomes yours.'

"We continued the work, ten years passed and the house became ours. We had it for a couple of years. But then Dennis started getting arrested for vigiling against war and nuclear weapons at Vandenberg Air Force Base. Some of the fines that were being given because he refused to pay were in danger of becoming liens against the house. We didn't want that. So the house went back to Larry in the form of a trust. But in essence it's ours.

"We've had food, shelter, clothing, medical care, music lessons for the kids. Along the line, we were made aware of private schools that we could never have afforded. But it turned out that none of the private schools really reflected our values. In this way as well, God curbs our appetites.

"We live within our means and absolutely, there's an abundance. We don't have payments. Most people have to slave over things they hate just to make payments. So our way leads to gratitude and a huge sense of freedom.

"There's another part. On the one hand, we don't want to incur debt and on the other, we also don't want to store up. Recently one of our volunteer doctors offered to pay for the expensive medicine needed by one of our patients. We said, 'Thank you, we're OK now so we can buy the medicine for him ourselves.' We felt we shouldn't take that money because at the moment we had enough. But see, that's counter to the thinking of most nonprofits. Any time someone wants to give money, the basic nonprofit philosophy is: *Take it! Thank you!*

"Personally, I don't think that's right. If we have enough money to pay our bills. and if we have enough money to do our work, if people offer us more I say, *No, give it to someone else who needs it.* There are plenty of other organizations who could use the money and we don't need it right now.

"I also get the hoarding in terms of emotional stuff. I have drawers-full and closets-full of letters. And the little knickknacks. The photos. Those I can't part with. But I didn't even realize that there are people who feel that way around money until seven or eight years ago when we did a Day of Recollection with the Newman Catholic Center at CalPoly. A woman who works in hospice came and gave us an assignment: Given six months to live, what are the five things you'd want to do and who are the five people you'd want to have in your life?

"You explore that. OK, three months have passed, now you have only three left. Finally, it gets down to your last week. What are the five things you'd want to do and the five people you'd want to have in your life?

"The questions are asked in a beautifully reflective way. You have your automatic responses and then you dive in. And I was amazed that people I really thought of as having a social conscience and a real depth of spirituality were talking about their retirement accounts! My IRA. 'I need that, my IRA.' I don't even know what an IRA is except that it's retirement money. Even as they're dying, how much money they have is that important to them.

"I felt that was emblematic of society. We're so consumed with having more money.

"Right when I was starting at the LA Catholic Worker, Jeff gave me an article called 'The Spirituality of Enough.' I loved that phrase. That seems so counter-cultural. Everything in our culture is about having more, wanting more, getting more, doing more. Last Friday's Gospel reading was about feeding the five thousand. The passage [see Matthew 14:13–21] says, 'They were all satisfied.' Everybody was filled and they were all satisfied. Part of that is this idea of 'It's OK.' We have enough. We're doing enough.

"But in our culture it's never enough. Even with Catholic Workers, sometimes the idea becomes, 'We're doing good service, people are sending money, so let's do more.' Our thinking is a little different. I was recently talking to some people from a sister house in Atlanta, Ed and Murphy from the Open Door, and I told them I don't feel like we've ever had a lot of ambition. We do our work and it's beautiful and it's enough. We don't have to cure all the ills or even attempt to. We don't need to do more and more. This is the work we've been given. These are the people we've been given. Let's just be faithful to that.

"So ours is a mindset that may not even hold sway in the Catholic Worker.

"The money comes in and it goes out. Our bookkeeping is very simple. It's all one pot in terms of the house stuff. Not long ago, Dennis actually started collecting Social Security so for the first time we've had money that comes to us that we live out of. Any food and clothes that we buy now comes out of our money. This is the first time we've had that in all our time together.

"Prior to that, Larry would give us three thousand dollars in a year. That was our personal spending money. The only part of donations we use for us personally is gas and bills. That's house money.

"What comes in Social Security is 1,300 dollars. It's incredible. It's funny, at first I thought, *What are we going to do with 1,300 dollars?* But teenagers, I don't know: twenty dollars here, thirty dollars there, the cell phone. Before you know it, my God, we'd used the 1,300 dollars.

"Because Dennis is older, the kids also get a small amount from Social Security. So, for the very first time in our lives, we have money coming in that we're not spending. We talked about it with the kids. We have discussions with the family over everything. Every expense gets discussed. Cell phones for the kids, any education kind of thing for them has always been discussed and now it's college. I wouldn't go get a job to pay for their college but on the other hand that money is there for them. Dennis is an older dad and there's a tradeoff. They don't have other benefits but they have that benefit.

"Just recently, last summer, I went to put gas in the car and the machine wouldn't take the debit card. I found we had maybe twenty dollars left in our account. So Dennis sent out a Christmas-in-July newsletter that month—the first appeal letter we'd written in eighteen years. Because we literally had nothing. People just started sending money. Right away we were fine.

"Every year I go to a hermitage in Snowmass [a Colorado monastery that takes private retreatants]. The only reason I'm allowed there is because I have a connection with Ladon. [Ladon Sheats was a fellow traveler, an ex-executive who'd given away all he owned and frequently stayed and worked with Catholic Worker houses across the country. Ladon was diagnosed with cancer and for four months in 2002 Tensie and Dennis, along with many members of the larger community, cared for him at their home until he died.]

"Every time I go there, to Snowmass, I feel like I'm almost on a chariot, being driven there by his love. Ladon had zero money and died with zero money. One time when I was there, oh my God, I realized, *This is my inheritance.* This is what he left me.

"And what could I *ever* want to leave now, to my own kids, but a connection, beginning with themselves, and then a place where they could go to foster, nurture, and dive into that? What could I *ever* want to leave them but a spiritual inheritance?

"The spirituality of enough comes with the knowingness of your belovedness. As I know him, you will know me" (see John 14:7). It's a flow that continues. It continued through Ladon. It flows through me. What you need, you will be given. You will be sustained. That might mean that your appetites might be curbed a bit. And thank God. You talk about how the desire for alcohol was removed from you. And I believe God graces us with freedom from appetites. With being content. That's not to say I have no appetites, I certainly love good food. I love a good bottle of wine.

"It's not a matter of being a Puritan. But I don't need that all the time. My life is fine.

"I'm a parent so I know how very much you want to give your kid good things. Ladon knew that. You couldn't pay me enough to work on Skid Row. You work on Skid Row out of love. Same with Ladon. What could he have ever left me in the way of money that would have meant anything?

"He gave me the place where he communed with God. He said in so many words, 'It's your turn now. And—pass it on.' That's the wealthy person. Just by virtue of being their friend, that's your ticket in. Look at Christ, who says, 'I no longer call you servants, I call you friends.' Being friends with Christ—that's our ticket in."

The Parable of the Talents (Matthew 25:14–30)

Tensie and Dennis show that the best way to assure being taken care of is to order our lives around service. When we ask on behalf of others, rather than ourselves, people always respond. When we focus our lives on helping others, we always get provided for, too.

But for me, that awareness has dawned very slowly. The parable of the talents, for example, is the one parable in the Gospels I'd never been able to get behind. My sympathies were all with the guy who got the one talent and knowing his master was a hard man who drove a hard bargain, buried his talent instead of investing it to make more. Here it is, for those who don't know it.

The Parable of the Talents

"For it is just like a man about to go on a journey, who called his own slaves and entrusted his possessions to them. To one he gave five talents, to another, two, and to another, one, each according to his own ability; and he went on his journey. Immediately the one who had received the five talents went and traded with them, and gained five more talents. In the same manner the one who had received the two talents gained two more. But he who received the one talent went away, and dug a hole in the ground and hid his master's money.

"Now after a long time the master of those slaves came and settled accounts with them. The one who had received the five talents came up and brought five more talents, saying, 'Master, you entrusted five talents to me. See, I have gained five more talents.' His master said to him, 'Well done, good and faithful slave. You were faithful with a few things, I will put you in charge of many things; enter into the joy of your master.'

"Also the one who had received the two talents came up and said, 'Master, you entrusted two talents to me. See, I have gained two more talents.' His master said to him, 'Well done, good and faithful slave. You were faithful with a few things, I will put you in charge of many things; enter into the joy of your master.'

"And the one also who had received the one talent came up and said, 'Master, I knew you to be a hard man, reaping where you did not sow and gathering where you scattered no seed. And I was afraid, and went away and hid your talent in the ground. See, you have what is yours.'

"But his master answered and said to him, 'You wicked, lazy slave, you knew that I reap where I did not sow and gather where I scattered no seed. Then you ought to have put my money in the bank, and on my arrival I would have received my money back with interest. Therefore take away the talent from him, and give it to the one who has the ten talents.'

"For to everyone who has, more shall be given, and he will have an abundance; but from the one who does not have, even what he does have shall be taken away. Throw out the worthless slave into the outer darkness; in that place there will be weeping and gnashing of teeth."

—Matthew 25:14–30 (NASB)

So as I was going about sympathizing with the guy who buried his one talent, a wealthy publisher offered to collect the essays I'd written for one of their magazines into a short book. Publishing is *a priori* stacked against the writer: the royalty split is generally around 88 percent to the publisher and 12 percent to the writer. That's always rubbed me the wrong way. The offered advance was also laughably small. My impulse in this case was to self-publish. Even if fewer people read the book. *I'd* have control. *I* could choose a decent cover for once. Even if I made less money overall, I'd get higher royalties on each book. Plus, why should a rich publisher get richer off *my* back?

I called my spiritual advisor and smugly laid it all out. As usual, I crowed, *I* had the courage of my convictions. I reviewed each point, emphasizing my clearly superior viewpoint.

"So I should say no, right?" I wound up.

He paused. "I'm feeling some anger there," he said. "I get what you're saying but after all, they're offering you something. They're saying, 'We *like* your work.' They're not against you, they're for you."

"I thought you were on *my* side," I sniffed, but I did take the matter under advisement.

That night around 3 A.M. I woke, sat bold upright in bed, and whispered: *The parable of the talents*! What skin was it off my back? If I had any gift of writing, the gift was from God. Once the work was finished, my job was to get it out to as many people as possible. As long as I was paid reasonably fairly, that someone else might benefit more than me was none of my business. I finally realized the point of the parable of the talents is that if you see God as a harsh master who drives a hard bargain, you're automatically *in wrong relation* with him. You're always going to be trying to outmaneuver him. You're always going to think you have to go to bat for yourself in the wrong way.

I do have to be wise in my business dealings. People, for instance, are often late in paying. I have to negotiate speaking fees, prices per word, methods and times of payment. We're in the world, and while we're not quite of it, I still have to tend to those things. I have to be on my toes. But when you give from the heart, in the deepest sense you don't count the cost.

You give because there's nothing you'd rather do.

PART TWO

THE LIE
The Law of Fear

CHAPTER TWO

MY OWN MONEY STORY

The first real story I ever wrote, in seventh grade, was about a princess who falls "madly, deeply in love"—not with one of the rich and charming men her wealthy father, the king, has picked out for her, but with a "lowly" gardener. The king, angry at his daughter's rebellion, orders the lover to be executed by drowning. The sentence is carried out. And the princess's response is to row out alone in her little boat, lower herself over the edge, and kill herself.

I called it "And Then—Darkness."

Before earning my first dime, I'd rejected wealth. Before my first kiss, I'd rejected the possibility of a romantic peer. Already, I'd decided not to accept largesse on the world's terms. Already, I "knew" the world would snatch from me what I'd worked hard for. Because of my terrible (and, given my childhood, not entirely unfounded) fear of rejection and abandonment (crossed with grandiosity, self-righteousness, and a host of other unsavory traits), already I'd developed a life strategy that, unbeknownst to me, was based on a lie; on a form of dishonesty with myself.

The lie was about the extent and the nature of my desire.

Here's how, in my working life, that panned out for me.

I left my job as an attorney in 1994. Still married, I'd squirreled away a couple of IRAs of about four grand apiece and a "nest egg" of twenty-eight grand that I put in a couple of mutual funds recommended by my (now late) father. For years, I would believe that money "enabled" me to write. I would believe that money was my hedge against working at another job that killed my soul.

Almost immediately I found freelance work, writing legal motions and briefs that paid first seventy-five bucks, and eventually ninety bucks, an hour. I worked only enough to pay my expenses, which at the time were minimal. My husband and I split the $700 monthly rent; I owned my car (a paint-peeling gray Mazda).

In 2003 I sold my first book for a $40,000 advance, and decided I didn't need to work freelance any more. I sold my second book in 2006 ($110,000), and my third book in 2009 (thanks, economic meltdown: $7,500).

Averaged out over the twelve years it took to write and publish those books, and minus the 15 percent agent's fee, that's $11,156 bucks a year. I made money other ways—selling essays, giving talks—but that whole time I was making and/or living on probably $20,000 a year. (According to a report by the California Budget Project, as of 2007 a single adult in Los Angeles needed to make $28,126 a year to live "modestly"). I also got divorced during that time, which meant that I lost the health insurance I'd had through my husband's job and my expenses doubled. Every so often I'd dip into my nest egg, but for the most part, there it sat. It did grow (though the market crash of 2008 wiped out at least a third), but there it basically sat.

And there I sat, too, working my tail off, obsessing about money, and thinking, *When am I going to be discovered? When is the windfall coming?* I did everything I could to promote my work. I went on a tour for my first book. I put up a website. I "joined" Facebook. I made it a point of discipline, pride, and love to respond to every e-mail from a reader.

But paradoxically, because I had the nest egg to fall back on, I wasn't particularly moved to earn; and because I was loath to spend any of my money, I might as well have had nothing.

CHAPTER THREE

VOLUNTARY POVERTY VS. COMPULSIVE POVERTY

Meanwhile, I steered social engagements toward coffee rather than lunch or dinner. I clothes-shopped at Goodwill. I had the same purse—a good purse, a $275 Donna Karan purse—but still, the same purse I'd bought fifteen years before while I was lawyering. I drove across country, twice, staying at Motel 6s, friends' houses, and monasteries. *I like walking around abandoned railroad tracks, freeway underpasses, warehouses, and vacant lots,* I kept telling myself. *I like the edges of things, the fringes, the high lonesome highway, the blue trail of sorrow.* I'm feeding my work.

All that was true, in its way, but it wasn't the whole truth. I was following my dream, to be sure, but over the years I also subconsciously adapted my dream to fit my fears around money. I eventually moved up from the Mazda (to a '96 Celica convertible). I eventually moved from ghetto Koreatown to a wing in someone else's huge beautiful house in Silver Lake (a hipster neighborhood in LA) that could have graced the cover of *Dwell*.

I'd developed a disciplined and authentic spiritual practice. I'd evolved to the point where, in my better moments, I *wanted* to be of service and to give of my gifts. I just couldn't believe that I was also "allowed" to make money.

St. Paul observed that love of money—note: not money, but *love* of money—is the root of all evil (1 Timothy 6:10). We tend to think "You cannot serve both God and mammon" means that we'll love money and hate God but it's just as bad to love God and hate money. If you hate something, you fear it. You don't want to look at it, you purport not to care what it's doing. And yet you're obsessed with it. You won't look it in the face, but you'll watch it like a hawk.

My spiritual bottom around money didn't consist in not being able to pay my creditors—I didn't have any creditors. My bottom wasn't realizing I lived in squalor; I lived in relative splendor. My bottom was realizing that something was fundamentally wrong, for a person who had graduated from law school with honors and passed three state bars; who could write, edit, speak, and teach; who was hard-working, well-organized, conscientious, and energetic, in seeing $900 as a livable monthly wage.

My bottom came in acknowledging that the way I lived invited me to be "brave" in some ways that were foolhardy, and in other ways not to be brave at all. My *primary* goal had become not to give all of my gifts but rather to conserve all of my money. My "living on the edge" was really living in the wrong kind of comfort, and the spiritual life calls us always out of our comfort zones.

What did I really want? I wanted to have faith in God—not in my nest egg. *What did I really want?* I wanted to be able to earn freely and spend freely. *What did I really want?* I wanted to stop giving money the wrong kind of attention.

When we start paying the right kind of attention, our strategies around money can yield startling discoveries.

"Absolute attention is prayer," observed the French intellectual-mystic Simone Weil.

In a way, this book is a prayer.

CHAPTER FOUR

UNDEREARNING, UNDERBEING

We can leave ourselves with too little money to share by overspending, over-sharing, over-giving. Compulsive generosity can result in its own kind of poverty.

We can leave ourselves with too little spiritual sustenance to share by failing to discern and/or to follow our vocation.

But those who are trying to live in voluntary poverty can go another way. Those who are trying to follow Christ sometimes engage in a strategy that, from an emotional-spiritual standpoint, encompasses the first two.

The phenomenon I want to present is what I'm going to call "underearning": a blanket term that includes but is not limited to self-depriva-tion, cash hoarding, and what I call "the poverty mentality."

While compulsive debtors use money as a drug, "underearners" use *lack* of money as a drug. Instead of *voluntary* poverty, our money life is one of *compulsive* poverty.

Underearners have developed an often subconscious, compulsive, strategy for thinking of themselves, and keeping themselves, perpetu-ally "poor." They take jobs below their level of experience and education. They've come to believe, all evidence to the contrary, that they have no marketable skills, that they can't make a living doing work they love, that money is antithetical to spirituality.

The upshot is talented, hard-working, good-hearted people whose lives, careers, and relationships never quite come together. Smart people who have ghettoized themselves, literally or figuratively.

In that sense, underearning is the psychic construct that underlies all money wounds. If we make loads of money and consistently blow it all, we leave ourselves at zero. If we're too afraid to follow the call of our hearts, one way or another we leave ourselves at zero. Underearning is perverse and it's progressive and it kills: dreams, spirits, lives.

I once heard a guy describe his job of thirty years: rodent exterminator. He said, "I'm maxed out on my credit cards, I'm in terrible financial insecurity, and I just don't understand why my business keeps going down. I have the most reasonable prices in the market. I try to be kind to my clients, often spending a few extra hours talking to an old lady or a guy in a wheelchair."

There's no shame in rodent extermination. But to undercharge and over-serve at the expense of providing for our own basic necessities isn't giving; it's using money—hoarding money, refusing to earn money, vagueness around money, thinking we're "above" or "below" money—as a form of anesthesia. A way not to feel, not to fully participate, not to face reality.

I don't want to pathologize normal human behavior. We'd hardly be human if we were neutral about money. To be fair, our whole culture is crazy around money. We talk about the economy, endlessly, but we don't talk about our strategies and fears around money. We complain about the price of health care, groceries, and gas but we seldom, if ever, talk about how much money we actually have, or how much we make, or how we decide to spend, or earn, or save. Artists in particular don't talk about money, except to corroborate one more time that we don't have enough of it.

We know money won't save us but how are we to make enough for the material things we decently, humanely need? How can we learn to be sane around money when we were never taught, and when many of us *have* been taught that to speak of money is unseemly? How can we live out the Gospel message, refrain from being greedy, and also let our desire, on all fronts, go to the stars?

CHAPTER FIVE

COMPULSIVE SELF-DEBTING IS NOT "A DESIRE FOR THE SIMPLE LIFE": IT'S INSANITY

I had certainly lived by the law of love when I'd quit Job B (lawyering) to follow my dream to Job A (creative writing). The work itself—the essays, the *All Things Considered* commentaries, eventually the books—had also always been fueled by love.

But when it came to money, I'd very quickly reverted to the law of fear. I had made one huge leap, yet I'd brought my hoarding/poverty mentality with me.

I'm willing to live close to the bone to do what I love, I kept telling myself. *I don't work for The Man. I've never sold out.* Maybe, but instead, I'd sold out to my shadow side, to my fear, to the generations of sorrow, shame, and financial insecurity that, like many of us, I'd absorbed along with my mother's milk.

The fear that there would not be enough money—anywhere, ever— came to permeate every aspect of my life. Here are some ways the fear manifested: Feeling an inordinate thrill over scurrying home with other people's cast-off clothing, furniture, or food. Walking a mile to save thirty-two cents. Doing things, going places, simply *because* they were "free." "Shaving off" money and time (e.g., "making up" for a parking ticket by deciding to live on crackers and cheese for a week). Not factoring in time to eat, rest, or pee during my day. A bizarre insistence on thinking of myself as underqualified for jobs for which I was in fact insanely overqualified. *Maybe I could get a job at the 7-11…*I'd think. *No, I probably couldn't figure out the cash register.* That was with a law degree.

There won't be enough money if on some basic level you refuse to *earn* enough money. Which can be obvious to the most casual observer—but entirely hidden from the underearner. And which is why the poverty mentality can manifest just as much in profligacy as in hoarding; just as much in overspending as it can in underspending; just as much in the midst of wealth as it can in the midst of scarcity.

I might not have owed anyone a penny. But I was taking more out of the world than I was putting in. That's a form of debt: not only to others, but to ourselves.

CHAPTER SIX

WE'RE INVISIBLY, IRREVOCABLY CONNECTED

A word here about mysticism. Mysticism means communion with an ultimate reality. Mysticism means realizing that our tiniest act has a supernatural dimension; that we are all intricately, integrally connected; that the bodies that house our souls are grounded firmly in the material world.

I'm a mystic—an ordinary one.

Mysticism is another way of saying that the law of the universe is love—and living by the law of love requires *taking action* in the concrete world. "Store up your treasure in heaven...for where your treasure is, there will your heart be also," said Christ, who knew better than anyone that we need to eat three times a day, find a bed for the night, and pay the doctor—and that the best way to be assured of those things is *to help the next person.*

The fact is no one is going to buy our movie or book if we're walking around thinking it's cool to look like FEMA victims. Or if they do buy our movie or book, we'll find a way to self-sabotage. Self-sabotage is the essence of underearning—of all forms of money dysfunction—which is why money is not remotely the main point. Money—hoarding it, not earning it, overspending it, obsessing about it—is simply one means we've found to mask the pain, live underground, and avoid coming fully awake.

Spirituality and money don't obey separate laws: across the board fear contracts; love expands. Underearning is toward isolation; authentic simplicity is toward community. Self-deprivation is toward power and control; authentic "paring down" is toward surrender. Compulsive poverty is toward chaos; authentic spirituality is toward healthy manageability.

Any kind of fear is against love—and when we're most in fear, we're least able to give. We want to be in communion with reality, because to be in communion with reality helps everyone, everywhere: past, present, and to come. We want to participate in the victory of love over fear.

Hoarding will keep us small; sharing will open a window upon the whole world. The idea is a current, a flow.

To freely spend secure in the faith that more will take its place: now *that's* mystical.

CHAPTER SEVEN

IT TAKES A LOT OF WORK TO STAY THE WRONG KIND OF POOR

As a child, I was mesmerized by Hetty Green. Billed in *The Guinness Book of World Records* as the stingiest woman on earth, Hetty lived in an unheated NYC apartment, ate cold oatmeal for breakfast, and had a son whose leg had been amputated because she was too cheap to pay a doctor. "The Witch of Wall Street" was pictured in a long black dress and matching cape of rusty baize. A sour look on her face, a roll of documents clutched in her hand, she was striding down a Manhattan sidewalk looking like she'd happily mow down any man, woman, or child who stood in her way.

At first glance, Hetty was no underearner—the Witch of Wall Street was also Wall Street's richest woman—but she still had the pauper mentality that whispers, *There will never, ever be enough.* She still used money as a way of altering reality, of making herself small, because deep down the underearning idea is that if you make yourself small enough nobody will be able to hurt you. *You can't abandon me, because I've already abandoned myself,* is the subconscious thought.

The actions harden into habits, the habits harden into compulsions, and each successive act digs the groove deeper, corroborates the twist of heart and mind that says, *See, no matter how hard I work, I need to work harder. No matter how much I have, I need to have more.* Other people get to prosper from their talents, but not me. I work and work, but I can never rest.

Underearning is a way not to feel, although paradoxically we are feeling—intense pain, loneliness, fatigue—all the time. It's a way not to be in reality, though, as with all compulsions, we're putting ourselves in a place that is far harsher, colder, and grimmer than reality.

Whatever form our money dysfunction takes, at some point, we have to ask ourselves, *What do I get out of it?* Because we do get something out of it—otherwise, we wouldn't engage in the behavior. In my case, I got to think: *My wants are different than normal people's. My needs are fewer. I don't participate in "the system."*

Early in my money recovery, for example, I spent a month in Palm Springs, housesitting for a friend. I had frequent phone chats with my new underearning friend Robert, even going so far as to tell him of my nest egg.

"Here's what I suggest," he said one day. "Set aside a certain amount of money, and go buy some stuff, specifically clothing, that's new."

"New!" I exploded. "I don't even need anything! I have a bunch of perfectly good clothes I found in the alley. I buy my stuff at Goodwill. People are always telling me how great I look. People are always complimenting me on my sense of style!"

But Robert, an inveterate thrift-store shopper himself, stood firm. "They call it currency for a reason. 'Current,' as in flow. What you're doing now you'll be doing ten years from now. You want to be open to a new experience."

This might sound New-Agey and weird but Robert was having a new experience himself, and I'd been following along with interest. He'd been saying things like, "I'm actually starting to feel like I belong for the first time in my life." Or "I've never wanted to be anything other than a marginalized, starving, loner artist. And you know what I'm seeing now? I'm seeing what I really want is to get married and have kids."

Getting married and having kids is possibly *the* lay-down-your-life-for-your-friends activity. When the student is ready, the teacher appears—even if the teacher is twenty years your junior. Thus I found myself one afternoon at the Desert Premium Outlets cruising the

Puma, Le Creuset, James Perse, Barney's New York, and Diesel stores. I'd assumed people who shopped malls were robot-like and shallow, with the same kind of grim, desperate faces you see in photos of people playing the slots in Vegas. To my astonishment, however, the folks by whom I was surrounded—Japanese couples, extended families, throngs of teenage girls—seemed to be having a blast.

Even more astonishingly, I, too, enjoyed trolling the wares. The Southern California sun beamed onto the courtyard. At the entrance of each store, I was welcomed, then left alone unless I needed help. I tried on a bunch of sneakers, lollygagged over the cookware, and ended up buying a very cool pair of True Religion (I liked the name) jeans.

The experience hardly made me want to go to the mall every day— once every few years still seems about right—but I had to admit that shopping retail was way easier, took way less time, and in the end was thus way less "expensive" than schlepping to ten different thrift stores. Also, I saw: *I had the money*. I was always going around saying "I can't afford it" and "I don't have the money," but in fact I *did* have the money. Why was being "poor" so important to me? Why was I so terribly loath to spend a few bucks?

The point is not to become a mindless consumer. The point is that in acknowledging that we have the same desires and urges as everyone else—to look good, to fit in, to be loved—we paradoxically become our authentic, unique selves.

What we do with the desires, how we choose to fulfill them, is ours. But to pretend we don't have the desires is an evasion and a lie.

CHAPTER EIGHT

THERE IS A SOLUTION

If the solution to my money issues were a class in financial planning, I would have been there, just as if the solution to alcoholism were a public-health class, I would have been there twenty-five years ago, too. But compulsive poverty is no respecter of intelligence, nor willingness to work, nor in many cases dazzling talent. It's a spiritual sickness, an emotional sickness, a twist below the level of consciousness whereby at some point the sufferer decides that self-deprivation is the solution to the human condition; that making do with less is the only way we're "allowed" to function in the world, to survive, or to do work that fires us up.

Whether our money issues center on overspending, underearning, or a crisis of vocation, the problem is vagueness and the solution, paradoxically, is not money, but rather clarity. Clarity around how much we spend (and on what), how much we earn, and how much (if anything) we owe. Clarity around our skills and their fair market value. Clarity around the fact that if we're self-employed, our most precious asset is ourselves, so we need to care for our health, pay ourselves a salary, and give ourselves sick days and vacations (!). Clarity around how we spend our time, on the difference between working and earning, on our goals, and on our vision: how we'd like our lives to look but maybe haven't quite dared.

The watchword is trust. The goal is to surrender to a power higher than ourselves. The underlying principle is love. We begin believing that the money *won't* "run out." We stop depriving ourselves in order to make someone else happy or out of fear that this is the one, last job; apartment; love interest; opportunity. We start paying back our creditors, if we have any, and we also treat ourselves to a movie or a wedge of good cheese or a nice bar of soap.

And while we're treating ourselves, we commit to a program of action that blows our usual strategies and schedule apart. We start devoting a few of those hours we would have otherwise worked for free to scoping out ways to earn. We find like-minded people, lay bare our money lives to one another, and start taking contrary action. (Why should we trust anybody, especially someone who has his or her own money neuroses? As a self-debting friend observed, "My mind's not out to get *you*. It's only out to get me"…). We can't think our way into right acting, but if we're lucky, we might just be able to act our way into right thinking.

The effect is of death and resurrection. We begin to die to our identities as "poor" people. We get glimpses of the childlike purity/openness of heart we had before the family patterns were blueprinted, or the childhood trauma occurred, or our own self-created wackiness intervened.

Let me emphasize: this is no quick fix. There are no quick fixes and no permanent fixes. There's progress, if we're open to grace, on a long, rocky road. There's fellowship and community. There are blinding flashes of joy and, as always in life, there's a whole ton of pain.

ACTIONS

We can't heal by ourselves.

After each section, I've listed some suggested actions that may help you get started as well. They're geared toward a combination of reflection, reading, writing, self-examination, daily tasks, and, always, community.

Setting aside the time to write and reflect; sharing my discoveries with others; and running my impulse to commit to a gig, make a major purchase, or tell someone to go to hell past a supportive friend first has gone further toward restoring me to sanity than I could have imagined.

1. Debtors Anonymous (DA) and Underearners Anonymous (UA) neither endorse nor oppose any outside enterprises, which of course includes this book. Still, twelve-step organizations are one logical place to start with respect to information, ideas, and community. As always, twelve-step programs are just one way to address the disease. As always, take what you like and leave the rest.

But so many people suffer from a variation of this condition, and I've suffered for so long myself that I'm thrilled to get the word out that the condition even exists. If just one person is encouraged to seek help for this potentially crippling illness—so much the better.

You can find Twelve Symptoms of Underearning at the website of Underearners Anonymous (www.underearnersanonymous.org/symptoms.html). Check them out and see if any fit.

2. Using free-form writing, describe the financial, emotional, and social condition of your family when you were born.

Then describe how your parents were around money through your childhood, adolescence, and up till the point you left home.

You *have* left home, right?...

3. Set aside fifteen minutes.

Write out how and where you usually shop for groceries, clothes, household items, and toiletries.

Now describe how you'd shop for groceries, clothes, household items, and toiletries if you had all the money you think you need, now and until you die.

4. List ten times you've deprived yourself in order to:

a) Pay back creditors;

b) Buy someone else a gift; and/or

c) Guard against guilt, shame, or the projected disapproval or anger of another.

TOOL:BOUNDARIES

I happen to be the type that people "love" to talk to. Which is fine, except that means I often end up listening to people with problems who have no intention of working toward a solution. Which is fine, except that I am very, very susceptible to taking on other people's burdens, other people's pain, and other people's unsettling dysfunctions.

I'm also the type that people tend to want to make their soul mate (never of course anyone I want to make mine). My fear in saying no— and in my experience, this is the fear of many underearners/codependents—is that I won't be "nice." I won't be kind. I won't be generous. But kindness consists in telling the truth, and the truth is that I have neither the time nor the inclination to become soul mates with complete strangers. "Don't engage" is my basic rule-of-thumb for the overly needy, snipers, and bullies.

To suffer with is compassion. That is always worth our time. To suffer because someone else wants to stay stuck is masochism. That is never worth our time.

Boundaries—knowing where I end and the other person begins—are all-important in recovery.

Check out any and all Al-Anon literature. These are people who have learned to make loving boundaries with drunks, junkies, crackheads, thieves, and neurotics of every kind. Who they also happen to be married to, have been raised by, or have parented.

They know.

STORY: STEVE D.

Steve D., forty-seven, is a gay performance artist and writer.

"My father was a doctor and my mother was a newspaper editor. I had one younger sister, and we bonded over being traumatized by my parents, especially around money.

"My father hoarded money and emotions and my mother was a spendthrift. She'd take us shopping and make us lie to our father about the things she bought. We'd be sitting in the driveway after a spree and she'd say, 'Don't tell Dad.' She made us her accomplices and she was also a bully. She'd get mad and say, 'You're stupid. You're ugly. No one likes you.' She arranged who I played with, spied on me, and laid out my clothes—Seriously! She was big on stripes—till I was fifteen.

"At the same time, she was totally hostile to my gayness. One of my earliest memories is of her screaming at me, *'Don't walk like a girl!'*

"At college I studied theater and multimedia performance art. My parents paid and I also had a trust fund I blew through pretty quickly. I'd go to lunch at the most expensive place in town—every day. At night, clubbing, drugs, drinking, anonymous sex.

"After the money ran out, I began working minimum wage jobs—dishwasher, copier. I always lived in the cheapest apartment in town, was always broke, was always scrounging, scavenging, and eventually stealing. Then I fell in with these 'artists' who were scammers. They had ways to get cheap cars, everything: shoplifting, home robberies. We were beating the system, I told myself. We were getting over on The Man.

"One night I picked up this guy at a bar and told him about my life of crime. I thought he'd be impressed but instead he said, 'That must be really hard for you.' I replied, 'You have no idea! I have to drive the car, I have to lie,…' And he said, 'No, no, I mean that must be really *hard* for you.' I said, 'Totally! It's a lot of work!' And finally he said, 'No, I mean looking into people's eyes while you're stealing from them must be *really hard.*'

"And I just started sobbing. Out of nowhere.

"So four years ago, I went into the money program [Debtors Anonymous]. Rigorous honesty, showing up and sharing in a group has been the most healing thing that's ever happened to me. I had no template for interpreting reality. My whole identity was tied up in being a victim. I'd been waiting for someone to rescue me instead of doing the work to take care of myself.

"I started to see that my problems around money stemmed from how I interacted with people. I had to learn how to make boundaries: *This is how I can have a relationship with you. This is how I can work for you.* I never knew how to say those things because I'd been too afraid to.

"Right around this time, I applied for a new job as a nanny. My friends in recovery said, 'What do you want from the job, and what are your boundaries?' So I raised my rate and I also laid out in advance what I would and wouldn't do. I wouldn't clean, for instance. My fear was that if I set boundaries, I'd lose the job—but the people hired me anyway! I had that job for three years. Loved the kid I took care of, never had a single resentment, and the woman I worked for ended up helping me find another job writing for a nonprofit.

"This was after a lifetime of looking at every boss I'd ever had and thinking, *What a jerk. I hate people.*

"With jobs since then, I've learned to have a conversation. I've taken courses in nonviolent communication. I still need tons of help, every day. But knowing I'm capable of asking for what I'm worth—and of *giving what I'm worth*—has changed everything."

PART THREE

COMING AWAKE

CHAPTER NINE

FROM FANTASY TO REALITY

Now that we know what underearning is, and have some rudimentary sense that we might suffer from a compulsion, we're called to come awake to the fact that it's not going to disappear on its own: in fact, as with all addictions, the untreated underearner gets progressively worse, never better.

Compulsive underearning is above all a disease of perception, a kind of willed, persistent fantasizing about getting from Point A to Point B with a huge yawning gap in the middle. *It will happen if I just stay in my room and think about it long enough*, the thinking goes. *If I keep my prices low people will see I'm a good sport and give me more than I asked for. If God sees I'm not asking for very much he'll think I'm good and not let anything bad happen to me.*

Interestingly, there's a "gap" when we take a leap of faith, too—that time we're in the air before we land on the other side—but that's a toward-life instead of a toward-death gap. That's a gap that is grounded squarely in reality. Dysfunction around money is grounded in fantasy, in winning the cosmic lottery, on getting results without stretching ourselves, taking a risk, or having to grow.

"When the unstoppable bullet hits the impenetrable wall," observes Robert A. Johnson in *Owning Your Own Shadow*, "we find the religious experience. It is precisely here that one will grow."

My own spiritual awakening had led me to Christ, but I had no illusions about his coming down off the cross to intercede. Christ worked through other people and especially, in my case, through the other sober drunks who, for twenty-five years, had alternately loved, annoyed, challenged, confounded, exasperated, healed, and filled me with wacked-out, wild-card hope. Working with other drunks had given me a blueprint for life that consisted in apologizing for my own part in a conflict, an ongoing examination of conscience, a basic stance of gratitude. Working with other drunks had led to a life ordered more or less to service, the ability to be present to other people, the capacity to ask for help.

Shining a light on my money "issues" wasn't an attempt, then, to bring out the big guns to solve a dilemma that my usual path wasn't up to. Rather, I was discovering that even doing work about which I was passionate, even a life basically ordered toward service was not enough. The problem wasn't that my blueprint was insufficient; the problem was that I needed to relinquish the entire purpose still essentially self-centered of why I was following it.

I was like the young man in Matthew's Gospel who approached Jesus and said:

> "Teacher, what good must I do to gain eternal life?" He answered him, "Why do you ask me about the good? There is only One who is good. If you wish to enter into life, keep the commandments." He asked him, "Which ones?" And Jesus replied, "*You shall not kill; you shall not commit adultery; you shall not steal; you shall not bear false witness; honor your father and your mother; and you shall love your neighbor as yourself.*" The young man said to him, "All of these I have observed. What do I still lack?" Jesus said to him, "If you wish to be perfect, go, sell what you have and give to the poor, and you will have treasure in heaven. Then come, follow me." When the young man heard this statement, he went away sad, for he had many possessions." (Matthew 19:16–22)

Of course that I should literally give everything away was a definite possibility. But even if I'd sold my stash of Goodwill threads, donated my beloved books and music to charity, and moved to Skid Row, the "possession" I wouldn't have been able to give away wasn't a material asset but my illusions: that money meant security, that I was in charge, that my peace of mind was dependent on my ability to manage and control.

How could I have done so much inner work and still be so sick? I'd never asked, "Why me?" about my alcoholism, my breast cancer, the drawn-out death of my father, my divorce. But I was asking it now, and the very asking was a sign that I needed to undergo another tectonic shift, the way I had when I stopped drinking: a movement from adjusting myself to what is rather than trying to tweak the world into being the way I wanted it to be; a movement from resistance to a new kind of surrender.

Simone Weil (1909–1943) was a French intellectual who'd insisted on working in a factory (though she'd been incompetent, loathed the work, and made no friends), was possibly anorexic, and upon volunteering as a nurse in the Spanish Civil War had promptly stuck her foot in a pot of boiling oil, causing burns from which she later, weakened by lack of food, fresh air, and human intimacy, died. Though drawn deeply to Christ, she refused to join the Church because she preferred to be in solidarity with the souls in hell: the patron saint of Those Who Do Things the Hard Way, a club of which I counted myself a charter member.

In her notebooks, Weil wrote: "Waiting patiently in expectation is the foundation of the spiritual life." Thanks, Simone. But maybe things weren't taking long at all.

Maybe if God could do things one second quicker, he would.

And maybe, just maybe, I could help things along myself.

CHAPTER TEN

WE ADMITTED OUR WAY WASN'T WORKING

Many of us are intensely antagonistic to the notion of "powerlessness." Let's be clear: powerlessness is not weary resignation, nor an infantile refusal to shoulder responsibility, nor a craven admission of defeat.

Powerlessness is a bold consent to reality.

It's accepting that the toaster is not *going* to fix itself: the toaster has been broken for two years and we need to buy a new one. It's consenting to see that fifteen grand a year is not a daring artistic statement; it's living below poverty level.

For my own part, I had that twenty-five years of sobriety. During that time, I'd done huge amounts of work on codependence, love addiction, and even money. I had what I believed to be, and still believe to be, an authentic spiritual practice that formed the ground of my life. That all counted; that all availed. But I had to admit one more time—which was hard, because I'd had to admit it so many times before!—that my way wasn't working. I professed to believe in a loving God, but I was obsessed with financial insecurity. I went around with a vague sense of unease that was so ingrained I'd almost ceased to notice it.

My views around money were so extreme and so distorted that an act of God—which is to say a radical paradigm shift—was required to restore us to sanity.

I'm a huge devotee of the Gospels. The stories there mirror my life back to me in unsettling ways. Take, for instance, the parable of the sower:

> Hear then the parable of the sower. The seed sown on the path
> is the one who hears the word of the kingdom without under-
> standing it, and the evil one comes and steals away what was sown

in his heart. The seed sown on rocky ground is the one who hears the word and receives it at once with joy. But he has no root and lasts only for a time. When some tribulation or persecution comes because of the word, he immediately falls away. The seed sown among thorns is the one who hears the word, but then worldly anxiety and the lure of riches choke the word and it bears no fruit. But the seed sown on rich soil is the one who hears the word and understands it, who indeed bears fruit and yields a hundred or sixty or thirtyfold.(Matthew 13:18–23)

"But then worldly anxiety and the lure of riches choke the word and it bears no fruit…". That was how my money issues manifested. I told myself I didn't care about riches, as no person bent on loving her neighbor as Christ loved us would, and yet I was obsessed with saving money. I wanted to bear fruit! I wanted to yield a hundred or sixty or thirty or even twofold by letting go—but surrender is a funny thing. We can't make ourselves surrender, but we are invited to show up in order to be open to surrender.

Surrender to what? To another way. To let a power greater than us be in charge as we continue to take action. To being transformed into someone and something we can't imagine because if we could imagine it, we'd try to manage and control and thereby sell ourselves short.

One thing I knew from those years of sobriety: Keep showing up. Keep desiring. Keep praying. Keep holding the tension between the way we wish we were and the way we really are; between the way we wish the world would be and the way the world really is.

And if we're having trouble admitting complete defeat, maybe we could think of it as a play on the word "admit," as in allowing entry to a place, fellowship, or community.

CHAPTER ELEVEN

WHEN WE DON'T TAKE CARE OF OURSELVES, WE SELF-DEBT

Who knew? Not setting aside money for taxes is self-debting. Not having health insurance *as a policy* is self-debting. If, after all good faith efforts, we're sincerely not able to pay our taxes or to afford health insurance, that's one thing. But to go without health insurance because we don't think we're smart enough to find work to pay for health insurance; or worse, as a kind of philosophical/political statement *when the real reason is fear*: that's underearning.

I've heard folks say that when they underearn, they self-debt. Personally, I self-debt whether I'm underearning or not; my impulse is to hoard and conserve no matter how much I'm making. I can keep meticulous accounts. I can get clear on the fact that my job is to spend more. I just have a very difficult time understanding, especially with a nest egg, that my job is also to *earn* more.

Partly this is because I tend to equate earning with spending time on things I don't want to do; for instance, marketing. As one of my heroes, the late comic Bill Hicks, said: "By the way, if anyone here is in marketing or advertising...kill yourself. Thank you."

Of course there's marketing as a corrupt, venal, life-sucking, lie; and marketing as a transferral of enthusiasm. I don't much enjoy either kind; partly because I don't think marketing will work for me, and partly because I would always, always, rather be writing. So I tend to be divided; I tend to feel like I'm "wasting" my time. And when I'm divided, I can't market with love. The key is to do everything with a hundred percent of my heart, which is to say with love.

Making an appointment for an eye exam, buying decent walking shoes, drinking plenty of liquids—small actions that *are* within my control, done with love—interestingly go toward what is not in my control, namely, my own transformation around money. The love leads to better earning, the better earning generates more healthy self-love, and pretty soon we'll all be lying around reading poetry to each other and raking in the dough.

Simple!

CHAPTER TWELVE

NO ONE IS GOING TO RESCUE US

Underearners always have one ace in the psychic hole: namely the thought: *If something truly bad happens, "someone" will take care of me.* In my case, this "person" was variously my ex-husband (so he had a new girlfriend), the county of L.A., or an order of kind, gentle nuns.

Most people facing the prospect of accident, injury, or illness, for example, enroll with Kaiser or Blue Cross. My health plan for many years was the Hawthorne Dominican Sisters. They were the people who'd cared for Mary Ann, the grotesquely facially disfigured young girl about whom the Catholic writer Flannery O'Connor had agreed, with much reluctance, to write a foreword for a book the sisters were putting together back in 1961 after Mary Ann had died, at the age of twelve, from cancer.

This is just the type of thing that appeals to me, so I googled the Sisters, found they still ran a place called the Our Lady of Perpetual Help Cancer Home in Atlanta, and checked out the application. Easy! Three pages and a note from your physician (I didn't actually have a physician but one would materialize when needed, I was sure, a Doctors-Without-Borders type who would be deeply impressed with my own life of giving). Super! I *liked* peaches and…what else did they grow in Georgia—pecans maybe? Great, liked them, too. My brother Joe (of the punk band the Queers), lived in Marietta and the sisters would be sure to have a chapel with the Blessed Sacrament. So that was my health care plan.

Similarly, most people when they want to buy a house apparently call a realtor, contact a mortgage broker, and start educating themselves about terms, points, and rates. This was my approach: for years I'd walk a shabby chic section of LA called West Adams thinking some old woman would see me wandering about with an interested cock to my head, realize that I appreciated the neighborhood, and will me her giant 1930s Craftsman with original moldings, hand-painted tile, and fir floors. "Why hello dear," I pictured her coming down off her wisteria-entwined porch one afternoon. "Would you like to fill in your name, D.O.B., and address and bring this codicil to a notary public?"

OK, so maybe I needed a little shift. So maybe what's interesting about recovery is that we need both (1) to be welcomed, accepted and loved just as we are and; (2) to discover that we are frightened, self-seeking, and deluded to the core.

But before we get to the second part, can I say something? We tend to excoriate ourselves these days for not taking "better care" of ourselves, but human beings aren't meant to take care of themselves all by themselves. This is the first time in history that men and women have been expected to live alone, in an apartment or house or room, and instinctively to know how to feed, clothe, entertain, comfort, and clean themselves while making every single decision solo.

So let's all give ourselves a break. And then let's get started on that shift.

CHAPTER THIRTEEN

WHO WANTS ME HERE?

Remember my underearning friend, Robert? It was Robert (again) who came up with this primo question to ask ourselves when we sense something is wrong but can't quite place whether it's us being insane or us starting to get well: *Who wants me here?*

For eighteen years, by way of example, I lived in a section of LA (that now has become, but at the time was far, far from "hip") called Koreatown. In many ways, I found myself in K-town. Those years were fruitful. Those years of solitude formed me as an artist. In many ways, those years served me. They were also years where I lived out some of my deepest misconceptions around money: that I could do what I loved but only if I remained poor; that I could live in a beautiful apartment but only if the apartment was in the ghetto.

At last I had to honestly ask myself—really, who wanted me in Koreatown? My friends didn't want me there: I'd put on these great dinners but the traffic was nightmarish and there was nowhere to park. After a certain amount of time, my landlord didn't want me there: he could have gotten way more than my increasingly below-market value rent. My neighbors didn't want me there, especially my downstairs neighbor who was a weasel coke addict, a pathological liar, and a DJ who would "warm up" for a Saturday night gig by blasting his odious bass-thumping "house music" starting at about four in the afternoon. God didn't want me there: He must have been thinking, *Why do you have to live in all that noise and traffic and far away from your friends when I want to give you everything!*

Most important, *I* didn't want to be there. I used to schlep around the 'hood, smiling hopefully at the armed gang-bangers, the teen mothers, the *paleta* vendors, the blank-faced Korean mom-and-pop store owners, thinking that I was learning to "detach"; that I was learning to "accept" because no one ever smiled back. Really, I was living in willed isolation among people who, by sheer dint of circumstance, were not my peers. Every time I heard another circling helicopter, street fight, or gunshot, I'd comfort myself by thinking, *I'm in solidarity with the poor*. Really, I was in solidarity with my terrible money fears.

My eyes must have roamed around that apartment—which really was beautiful—a million times: the crown moldings, the hardwood floors, the courtyard. *I'll never find another place like this*, I thought. That thought kept me trapped. That thought kept me paralyzed, like the crippled man in the Gospels (John 5:1–18) who'd been on his mat by the pool for *thirty-eight years*.

When I finally moved (a story in itself), I didn't even have to look for another apartment. A friend recommended me to another friend who rented me a wing of her huge beautiful house with Wi-Fi, a washer and dryer, parking, a gazebo, and a gigantic backyard in Silver Lake, my dream neighborhood, where I *pay less than I did in Koreatown*.

Who wants me here now? I do.

CHAPTER FOURTEEN

THE WAY WE ARE WITH MONEY AFFECTS THOSE AROUND US

Chances are that if we're spending zero money on entertainment, zero money on health care, and zero money on vacations, we're also spending zero money on gifts. Or if we are spending on gifts, it's begrudgingly, even if we desperately don't want to be begrudging.

This is the where the faux-revolutionary cry of addicts of all stripes rears its lying head: to wit, *It's* my *life, I can do whatever I want with it.* If I want to kill myself, that's my choice. If I want to live on twenty-seven cents a day, that's not hurting anyone else.

Well, yes and no.

Living on twenty grand or ten grand or five grand a year is fine if (1) you have no other choice; or (2) the decision to do so is consciously born of freedom, joy, and an expansive desire for community.

But if bringing in a certain (meager) amount of money becomes the end rather than the means, something's wrong.

If you're adapting your wants to fit your compulsion, rather than adapting your earning to meet your wants, something's wrong.

If you got a windfall and would be unable to share it, as people who live in freedom and joy would be able to do, something's wrong.

If you work all the time and would work even if you didn't make enough money to humanely live on at it, something's wrong.

If your focus is on how to get something for nothing, something's wrong.

During the month I was staying at my friend's very cool all-white Alexander mid-century place in Palm Springs, for example, I happened to be snooping around in the medicine cabinets, just checking things out. *Oooh, lots of skin lotions and cream. Oooh, here's a blue jar of Egyptian Dead Sea Mud. Oooh, way in the back.* She *never uses it…I should use it…*

Now mind you, I'd brought my own skin cream. But such is the crafty money-fearing mind that if the tiniest chance to "conserve" (your own stuff, and use someone else's) presents itself, you will.

So having just emerged from the shower, I gingerly dabbed on a bit of Dead Sea Mud (hoarders generally don't slather, even other people's products). Suddenly I thought of my friend's unfailing generosity, of the way she'd offered me the master bedroom, of how, as she was leaving, she'd said, "Feel free to help yourself to the (fully stocked) cupboards, fridge, freezer…"

And my next thought was: *Buy your own freakin' Sea Mud.*

Sometimes shame is a good thing.

CHAPTER FIFTEEN

HUMAN FREQUENCY

"He travels fastest who travels alone" had for years been my credo. *People slow you down,* I told myself. *People are messy. People want things from you.* Which may be true in one way, but is not true in all ways.

Because even us die-hard introverts can't heal on our own. Because at some point the question becomes: Where are we traveling *to?*

The word *companion* comes from the Latin *cum pane*: "with bread." Companions are as essential as bread. Companions will move us forward. Making more money is lovely, but companions will share our heart.

That being said, I don't do community well, our culture does not do community well, and LA in particular does not do community well. Then again, the problem—I can only speak for myself—may be pride. To admit "I'm a grown woman or man and I can't stop watching Internet porn, or scarfing Vicodin, or squirreling away every spare penny" requires a terrible vulnerability. To ask for help, invite people in, or show up in any way beyond our immediate comfort zone means taking an extreme risk.

Here's an extreme risk I took shortly after beginning this work: I conceived of the idea to get together a monthly roundtable of artists. Having *longed* for creative community, I was quite proud of myself. For three months running, I spent seventy bucks or so of my own money and several hours preparing. I shopped, I cleaned the house, I cooked, I hummed with happy expectation, I cleaned up after.

The first time was great. The second time was pretty great. The third time people didn't bother to answer the invite, people e-mailed ten minutes after the thing had started to say they couldn't come, people texted in the middle to say "I'm lost" (my place is not remotely hard to find), and then showed up without the dessert they'd promised to bring.

I quietly realized that for whatever reason (I should say that, not wanting to be a "snob," I'd let a couple of people come who weren't strictly in the creative arts and were in fact borderline personality or drunk), my precious plan, my *brave* plan, was not to bear fruit.

With my "tortured sensitivity," I could have shut down to any notion of community. I could have succumbed to my wounded pride. I could have felt pathetic and sorry for myself.

Instead, I realized how dear my friends had been to show up with all the good food, good cheer, and ideas for good art that they had.

I thought, *Let me try something else.*

I started writing this book.

ACTIONS

1. Make a list of five things you've been telling yourself you're going to do for over a year: cleaning out the garage, getting a dental implant, taking a weekend road trip. Then get really quiet, summon up all your courage, and take a small first step toward doing one of them.

2. List ten situations and/or personal characteristics in your life that, by yourself, you have the power to change. Then, list ten that, by yourself, you don't.

3. What compensatory action(s) do you take, if any, when you:
   a. Get a parking ticket.
   b. Learn of an unexpected car repair.
   c. Have a medical situation, however minor.
   d. Hear the stock market is crashing.
   Why? Do the actions help? If not, what is their actual effect?

4. List five ways in which you've been thinking, perhaps subconsciously, that if push comes to shove, someone will rescue you. If *at least* five don't immediately jump to mind, consider your living situation, family situation, relationship situation, career situation, and health/dental/car situation. Really?

5. Do five minutes of free-form writing on one primary situation in which you feel trapped. Ask yourself: Who wants me here? If no one does, why are you still there? And if people do want you there, *why are you putting their desires above your own?*

6. List the last five gifts you gave, of either money or material goods. Then do some free-form writing around each. Discuss your thought processes, plans, schemes, hopes, fears *before* giving the gift. Did you obsess over: how much it cost; whether you should pay to have it wrapped (of course not, then used a cut-up brown paper grocery bag and a salvaged scrap of Christmas ribbon—in July); what did the person ever buy you?.

Discuss your feelings *after* giving the gift. Did you "re-purpose" not as a way to save the environment but as a way to avoid spending money? Did you burn with shame, realizing afterward that the other person probably didn't want a bar of chemical magnolia soap and a Starbucks promo cup either?

Start gearing up to buy your friend, whom you love, a decent gift next time. Something brand new. From the store. That you've thought about, planned for, and looked forward to. Because it's for them. But in some weird way, it's also for you.

7. Guesthood and hosthood both require risks. If you're a perpetual guest, for once be a host. You get to figure out how and under what circumstances. If you're a perpetual host, for once leave your comfort and control zone, accept someone else's invitation, and consent to be a guest. Bonus points if you take a risk, either way, and the thing falls flat.

TOOL: BOOKENDING

Bookending is calling or texting someone (1) before you're going to, say, make a difficult call, make a large purchase, or negotiate a deal; and (2) calling the person after.

It's a way of not doing everything in frightening isolation. It's a way to remember that we're in community and have friends and supporters. It's a way of learning that others often have perspective, jokes, suggestions, and a surprising ability to ground us.

Try this. Take a friend out to lunch. If coffee is all you can afford, take him or her out for coffee. Estimate how much the outing will cost, including tip. Call someone before, tell them the max you plan on spending, and note your feelings. Then call them after. Again, note your feelings.

Refrain from thinking, "I'm thirty or fifty or ninety years old and I'm going to *call someone and report that I'm taking a friend out for a forty-five–dollar lunch?*" Yes, you are. Because money stuff is triggering to you. Because you love yourself and you want to get better.

STORY: VALERIE V.

Valerie V., forty-two, works in the downtown LA fashion industry.

"I have a long history of underearning that includes serial evictions and a mid-90s bankruptcy filing. It's taken years of recovery but now I drive a newish BMW, have an apartment I love, and thrive as head of accounting (I was promoted last year) for a high-end shoe company. I get to fly to the Paris fashion shows and last week my boyfriend and I had dinner at a fundraiser at Alice Waters' house. I also take ballet lessons—actually, I'm obsessed with ballet, which I have to keep an eye on, because that can run into some cash, not to mention time. I'm in a long-term relationship with a guy who lives on a trust fund. He's a teacher and though he *has* more money, I actually *make* more money than he does. I actually think he's kind of cheap, which we've had to work out over the years.

"That all sounds very la-la but I'm really clear that it's not the apartment and job and car in and of themselves that make me happy. I'm also very clear that, left to my own devices, I'm forever in danger of being two hundred dollars short, no matter how much money I make. So I stick really close to the program and to my sponsor. I accept that I need help with things that other people master at about the age of eight.

"Last week, for example, I wanted to buy a new bed. Now in the old days I would have gone shopping, fell in love with a bed that was way too expensive, had it delivered, and then discovered it wasn't even the same size as my headboard and mattress. So this time, before going to Ikea, I measured, wrote everything down, and even brought a tape measure.

"I was still totally overwhelmed. So I called a friend in recovery from the store and she walked me through. 'What's your spending plan?' 'Will the bed you want go with your room?' 'No, you don't need to buy a matching dresser, armoire, bookcase, and bedside table *today…*'

"I bought my bed that day, and that night I cooked dinner for three young women I know who are newly sober. I'm going to help another put in a vegetable garden next weekend.

"So you earn and you spend. You get help and you give help. You're part of life instead of cowering in the corner wondering if your electricity is going to be shut off."

PART FOUR

FORENSICS

CHAPTER SIXTEEN

CLARITY WITH NUMBERS

I used to be clear beyond belief on, say, the price of a gallon of milk at five different grocery stores, but completely vague about how I proposed to live indefinitely while earning three hundred dollars a month.

The solution for vagueness is clarity.

Clarity—in fact all the principles in *Loaded*—apply across the board, to every area of our lives.

Numbers want to be free, to multiply, to support. Numbers have their own magic. Numbers want us to be clear with them. Let's start on getting clear with:

1. How Much Do I Need Every Month?
2. How Much Do I Make/Earn Every Month?
3. How Much Debt Do I Have?
4. How Much Do I Want to Make?

At first, I totally balked. Such questions made me feel cornered. Why would I want to keep such ridiculously minute track of my money? I had a giant (relative to the way I lived) nest egg! I'd rather be writing. I'd rather be looking at the flowers and the trees.

Fair enough, but a certain portion of my writing and looking at the flowers and trees was driven by the fact that subconsciously I was in so much pain and bewilderment around money. I worked all the time but the money didn't seem to come in.

At the suggestion of a friend in recovery, I started writing down every penny that came in, whether through earning or otherwise, and every penny I spent. When I started getting clearer about what I needed and what I made, what had seemed insurmountable became finite, right-sized, smaller than me. The numbers were not my master. The numbers did not contain my childhood. The numbers were not freighted with metaphysical significance about my intrinsic worth, the odds of failing, or the amount of love in the world.

I didn't understand how or why, but my willingness to take the simple action of "keeping my numbers" led toward a shift.

Here's an example: through a writing gig I'd gotten through a friend of a friend, I read an article about being a sober companion. Now heretofore I wouldn't have touched such a thing with a ten-foot pole: a useless hack job, in my mind, invented to fleece rich people.

But after mulling for a bit the idea came: why not call a priest friend who works at Betty Ford and ask his advice? So I called Tom and he didn't know anything about sober companions but he did say, "Sounds like you could do a lot of good—why not look into it?" And then he proceeded to tell me of Fr. Frank Sabatté, a New York City priest who'd started an arts collective to explore the connection between mystery, transcendence, and art, and who was a crazy good *portrait embroiderer.*

So I called Fr. Frank; he agreed to an interview, and I got to post about him and his work on my blog.

And right after that, I got an offer to teach the Master Rewrite Class at a place called the LA Writers Lab.

Meanwhile I forgot all about the sober companion gig, which I realized afterward in fact would not have been my thing at all.

"Polish over here and it'll shine over there."

Real wealth consists in a wide circle of acquaintances and friends.

CHAPTER SEVENTEEN

CLARITY WITH TIME

Here's a question you may or may not ever have asked yourself: Where does my time go?

If you haven't, you really might want to start. I used to love to troll eBay, for example, for "re-purposed" Linea Pelle belts, Arche boots, and Cydwoq sandals. With the hours I spent obsessively comparing, and checking back, angling to save five bucks, I could have written and sold a whole essay, thereby making enough money to buy a *new* belt or pair of shoes.

"Me Time"

"Me Time" is one of my friend Robert's more brilliant concepts. Here's his description of a typical pre-recovery evening: "On the (two) days a week I worked, I couldn't wait to get home. On my way I'd stop at the Thai place—I had to get this one special item. Then in my room, I'd arrange everything around my computer like a shrine: Thai food here, Diet Coke there, candy, phone. And I'd settle in to watch two or three Netflix. Hours would pass. It would be like I was drugged. I felt nothing. And then, finally, I got to go to bed…"

There's nothing wrong with a night, or even many nights, to ourselves. There's nothing wrong, in and of themselves, with takeout, Netflix, Diet Coke, or relaxing. But when that kind of zoning out becomes the focal point of our lives; the reward for a few begrudging hours of "participating"—that's when we cross over from healthy to unhealthy "Me Time."

Huge chunks of my life have been geared toward getting everybody and everything out of the way so I can look forward to an uninterrupted stretch of *time to myself*, like a miser with her pile of gold. Just as I "hoarded" money, I realized, I had a tendency to hoard time!

On the other hand, as a writer, I legitimately need quiet time in order to work. Also, I'm an introvert, and I'd do violence to myself in trying to change that. Many of us are solitary by nature and temperament. We need alone time the way we need air and light and water. But to use solitude as a *drug* isn't good. We don't get to withdraw from the world out of sloth, fear, or despair and then call ourselves "contemplative."

We do get to move toward change, and what's interesting is that the changes can, maybe should, be quite small. The simple discipline of making one "outreach" call a day, of factoring in coffee with a friend twice a week, of committing to a twelve-step group for, say, a year, can transform our attitude; our whole orientation of heart.

That is not New Age, self-help, or woo-woo. That is part of the network of small instances of shared gifts and community that are not only life-affirming, but that constitute life itself.

Time Squatting

"Time squatting" is metaphorically putting fifty beach towels out on the sand every morning and feeling compelled to lie down on every one of them: towels labeled, for instance, "Pharmacy, oil change, visit elderly mother, write for four hours, bake cookies, clean out garage, get teeth cleaned, embroider tablecloth for child's baptism, meditate, exercise, save world…"

Give this a try: If you *never* make a to-do list, make one. Observe what happens and how you feel. If you *always* make to-do lists, refrain for a week. Observe what happens and how you feel.

Have a rough idea of how you want your day to go and what you want to get done. Then let the darned thing unfold.

CHAPTER EIGHTEEN

CLARITY WITH WORKING VS. EARNING

Every individual soul…like every individual machine or organism, has its own best conditions of efficiency. A given machine will run best under a certain steam-pressure, a certain amperage; an organism under a certain diet, weight, or exercise. You seem to do best, I heard a doctor say to a patient, at about 140 millimeters of arterial tension. And it is just so with our sundry souls: some are happiest in calm weather; some need the sense of tension, of strong volition, to make them feel alive and well. For these latter souls, whatever is gained from day to day must be paid for by sacrifice and inhibition, or else it comes too cheap and has no zest.

—William James, *The Varieties of Religious Experience*

Now that is me to a T. Whether from genetic blueprinting, my childhood, or a combination of the two, I tend toward the austere and ascetic. I like things to be difficult. Nothing wrong with astringency except when it crosses the very thin line between passion and pathology. I used to run myself ragged, for example, scurrying around town looking for "a bargain." Hungry, angry, lonely, and tired, some days I felt my whole life was one long obstacle course.

I finally realized that to spend half the day writing (and not making enough money), and the other half trying to get the best price on a bag of carrots wasn't the best use of my time, energy, or intelligence. I finally realized, *Just buy the freaking razors, skin cream, toilet paper,* and *milk at Rite-Aid.* I finally realized, *Just pay the fifty cents for parking instead of circling the block for twenty minutes like an insane person, the whole time thinking,* I'm going to be late and I have to pee.

I finally realized that blowing two hours to save three bucks is actually working—for a buck-fifty an hour.

Let's also distinguish between work as a neurotic, grim expenditure of labor and time (often on something that doesn't interest us and is also of no real use to the world) and work as an outgrowth of passion, at which we will (rightfully) expend any (even outwardly insane) amounts of time and effort.

Earn a humane living. And give to the world your whole hemorrhaging, anguished heart.

CHAPTER NINETEEN

CLARITY WITH RESENTMENTS

Resentments suck us dry of the very energy we could otherwise use to make the changes that would make us feel better. Our desire to get even with those who have hurt us can be dark, deep, and borderline crazy.

Resentment means "to feel again." Wasn't once enough?

One solution is to take a long, hard look at our resentments, and to do some writing on them. Here's one format, pretty much straight from the 4th Step of Alcoholics Anonymous, that works well.

For each resentment, write:

1. I'm Resentful at (Name the Person).

2. List the Reason(s).

Get down to it. Get really, really honest. You're pissed at your roommate because she made a snide comment when you cooked a cheeseburger for breakfast. You're pissed at your mother, who's been dead for twenty years, because she never told you were pretty. You resent him because he'll sleep with sex workers but he won't sleep with you.

Next, we move on to the areas of our lives that the resentment affects.

3. The Resentment Affects My:

Choose one or more of the following or fill in your own: Self-Esteem, Ambition, Security, Identity, Career, Personal Relationships, Sex Relationships, Wallet. The idea is to uncover why we feel so threatened, afraid, challenged, or angry at this person.

4. Where Was *I* (Leaving Aside the Other Person) Selfish, Dishonest, Self-Seeking?

Write it out. Again, be ruthless.

5. Telling It to Another.

After you've listed and broken down all your resentments, find someone who's as nuts as you and you read your list to that person. I always *feel* this won't work. But this simple willingness to open myself to another human being, even while I'm sure the whole time she's thinking about whether she should move her desk and the color of her new lipstick has proved transformative.

Acting charitably toward the person you resent, even though you're still pissed, also works. I once had the supposedly huge honor of being "interlocutor," for example, in a public conversation with a best-selling author. I carefully read this woman's book and prepared my questions. I prayed for her, I showed up on time, I privately considered myself an ambassador for the city of LA and the noble cause of writing. And this gal barged in late, with a huge noisy entourage, was grotesquely rude, and turned the "conversation" into possibly the most unpleasant hour and a half I have ever spent, which is saying something.

In a state of high dudgeon, over the course of the next year I retold the same moth-eaten story a half-dozen times, which of course only reflected badly upon me. Then out of the blue one day I received an e-mail from a reader saying how kind the writer in question had once been to her. And instead of replying, "Well she was a total witch to me and her book sucked, too," I wrote back, "How beautiful so-and-so was kind to you." *Period.* The resentment melted.

And here's the thing: afterward, I realized I wouldn't have felt quite so insulted if I hadn't wanted something in return from this woman: possibly the recognition, in light of my own enormous talent, of my *incredible* and very becoming modesty. I probably wouldn't have held on so long if the writer hadn't been famous. In other words, I was *jealous.* I don't know about you but I will call jealousy just about anything other than actual jealousy. *Jealous—please! Jealous—me?* I would not stoop to jealousy. Except I'm jealous.

So I called my spiritual mentor and laid it all out, including the all-important "my part."

After the fact, and about a year too late, but still. We cracked up. We marveled at the underlying spiritual principles of honesty and forgiveness.

Thus, the beauty of a moral inventory.

ACTIONS

1. Get quiet for fifteen minutes. Look over the coming month. Ask yourself: In order to maintain the flow of money in my life, what action do I need to perform...

    a. this month?

    b. this week?

    c. today?

We don't have to take the actions today with the goal of being financially safe *forever*. We build up a prudent reserve (say, three months' worth of expenses), if possible, and then we go along month by month. Let the old, outworn, and useless go. Let the new flow in.

2. Keep a time log. Just for five days, just for the heck of it, keep track of how you spend your time—down to the minute. Note: When did I earn? (if at all). Note: "Unhealthy Me Time." Am I connecting with "old tapes," for example, People are dangerous, People slow me down, People cost money?...

3. Create a flexible time plan. Factor in time to earn and also factor in time to do what you love, what makes you happy, what replenishes you. Not what the marketplace tells you to consume, not what the world tells you to crave, not what the culture ridicules, shames, and frightens you into doing—but what you love.

4. Think of a time when you gave that made you feel so, so good. What was it that you gave? Meditate for fifteen minutes on how you could give that thing again—possibly as a livelihood. Then spend fifteen minutes writing down the thoughts that come up.

5. Off the top of your head, list five resentments (remembering that resentment means "to feel again"). Use the format described on page 66 to write them out.

6. Find a friend who's willing to listen to you and read your inventory, the whole thing, just as you wrote it. Then pray for the people on your resentment list every morning for two weeks. Pray that they get everything that you want for yourself: money, success, happiness, love, a parking spot at Trader Joe's.

As Blessed Charles de Foucauld (1858–1916) said, "Let's ask together, for every human being, what we ask for ourselves."

TOOL: KEEPING OUR NUMBERS

Get yourself a Moleskine or other cool, classic notebook and a fine-point pen. Or do your new-fangled smart phone thing if you must. Whatever the case, start keeping track of every penny you spend and every penny that comes in. If you spend a quarter for parking, write it down. If someone gives you a twenty-buck gift card for your birthday, write it down. If you get a $1.98 refund, write it down.

You can go on to categorizing, Excel, separate accounts for business and personal, and your own personal CPA later. But start with this.

Every penny. Every day.

STORY: FIONA T.

Fiona T., fifty-three, does research and devlopment for a small start-up tech firm.

"I work for the woman who started and owns the company. It's just her and me and, though she referred to us as partners, after a couple of years, I started to totally resent her! She worked fewer hours than me and made way more money. My impulse, under the guise of 'honesty' was to *tell* her I was upset. But as a friend said, 'What is she supposed to do with that? Say, "Thank you for reporting that you don't like me?"'

"That same friend told me about DA. I'm not an alcoholic, though there's lots of alcoholism in my extended family. I'm not a huge debtor. But I'd always been a follower, not a leader—and not in a good way; in a standing-in-the-shadows way. So though I'd never been involved with any step program, I went with my friend to a meeting, and something clicked.

"I began to see I'd always been in a certain amount of chaos around money. I'd overspend and then get weirdly obsessed with 'finding a bargain.' I'd fish the newspaper out of the bin at Starbucks rather than shelling out a buck-fifty, then spend forty bucks on dinner—even though I had a full refrigerator at home. I'd either shop impulsively, or I'd visit twenty different stores and be unable to settle on *any* sofa or lamp or car. I'd be afraid of making a mistake, committing, being disappointed...

"At first I started 'keeping my numbers' just to go along. It seemed not to make any sense—how was that going to help that I wasn't crazy about my job or my boss? But getting clear, being adult enough to look my money in the face, made me realize how much I had avoided in my life simply through staying vague. I was vague about how much money I earned and spent, vague about what I really wanted out of life, vague about the constant, low-level resentment and hostility I felt toward people who were 'doing better than me.'

"I talked over my resentments with my sponsor and I finally realized I'd signed up for exactly the job, hours, and pay I was receiving. My partner wasn't ripping me off. She wasn't paying me less than I was worth. I was just pissed and jealous that she was making more than me! If I wanted to start my own company, with all the risk and responsibility that entailed, I could do that myself. Otherwise, I could try to do the best possible job with her and for her. My anger lifted. And a couple of months later, without ever having had a conversation, she 'spontaneously' offered me shorter hours and more money. Our relationship underwent a strange and unlikely shift.

"The shift has sent out ripples. I'm planning a trip to Istanbul with a couple of friends. I put in a deck at my house. My family's been coming over more. Family...now that's *another* program..."

PART FIVE

HEALING

CHAPTER TWENTY

RIGHT-SIZING TRAUMA

I could write a book—in fact, I did write a book; it's called *Parched*—about the way our childhoods, in particular, the way we interpret them—shape our psyches, hearts, and destinies.

The self-rejection starts early. We "should" be someone else. We "should" have known. We "should" have been born into a different family, in a different state, country, century, geological age; with a different gender, sexual orientation, type of hair, body.

The spiritual journey consists precisely in uncovering these subconscious motives, drives, and old ideas. And every second of our lives, every iota of effort we've put toward coming awake already has "registered." Nothing has been lost, nothing has been wasted; everything we've done to walk toward the light has been preparing to bring us to the point where we're willing to change in a new and different way.

Often, in what seems a cruel twist of fate, we're on the way to fulfilling our dreams and some ghastly setback occurs: a rejection, an abandonment, an accident, an illness. "Look," our inner voice whispers, "things were looking up and this is what happens. You fail. You stumble. You fall. So stay small, stay safe." Out of love, our egos want to protect us from getting hurt again. But we don't want to stay stuck in the desire to avoid hurt all our lives. When we right-size the trauma, maybe we can start to move on.

The first, and really only, time I was poised for "a big life" was around the age of twelve. As a kid in elementary school I was a straight-A student, an athlete, a "leader." In eighth grade, I was chosen to compete in the prestigious Oratorical Contest and that's when my forward momentum came to a screeching halt. I memorized the speech so as not to mar my delivery by so much as the rustle of a turned page, and the night of the event, lost my place, stood silent for what seemed like an eternity before practically the entire assembled small town, stumbled, failed. That I went on to graduate valedictorian of my class didn't matter. That I won the coveted American Legion Award didn't matter. I'd had my chance and I'd blown it. I was tainted, in my mind, for life. I'd always known that happiness, love, and money were "for other people" and now I had proof.

Decades after the fact, I reprised the Oratorical Contest in my first book. I relived the sweat trickling down my side, the second-hand of the clock ringing out like pistol shots, the sense that the crowd might rise up and begin stoning me, like the townsfolk in Shirley Jackson's "The Lottery." Somehow the reliving, the writing, the seeing myself as a darling, brave twelve-year-old girl, constituted a kind of exorcism.

Trauma works itself out through our bodies and psyches on its own time. The scars remain. But now I'm sure that not one person in the town of North Hampton, New Hampshire, remembers the 1966 Oratorical Contest and if they do, I'm positive—positive!—he or she doesn't hold it against me.

I'm positive that I'm now allowed to earn.

CHAPTER TWENTY-ONE

THE PACTS HAVE EXPIRED

"How glibly we talk about 'family-life,' as we do also of 'my country.'
We ought to say many prayers for families. Families frighten me.
May God be merciful with them."
—Georges Bernanos, *The Diary of a Country Priest*

Many of us feel a deep loyalty to our (possibly dysfunctional) families of origin and to our place in them. "Parents eat sour grapes, but the children's teeth are set on edge" (Ezekiel 18:2). Family trauma has been found to affect the next seven generations down the line, even when no additional trauma occurs.

I can sincerely say I had the best parents in the world. Like all parents, they also had their stuff. My mother saved slivers of soap in an old shortening can under the sink. My father, a bricklayer, spoke, often, of a place called "the poorhouse." Financial anxiety ran like a live electric current through our house: across every doorway, straight down the middle of the dining room table, around the edge of the flimsy mattress while you tried to sleep.

We never actually went hungry in my family, but we went unsatisfied. Five pork chops for seven people. For Christmas one year my "big" present was a blanket. I felt shame at the meager portions my mother served to friends when they came over for supper, and more shame that she didn't know to be ashamed; didn't see we were weird. I felt the shame of not knowing how to communicate; of having feelings that could not be given voice. *I hurt. I long. I want to help. I love you.*

We rarely went to the doctor (too expensive, plus, grin and bear it). We had our teeth drilled without Novocain (Novocain costs). Doctor's visits were reserved for broken limbs, burst appendixes, or gashes sufficiently severe to require stitches. The message I picked up there was: *You can't afford to be helped, and when you can, the help hurts.* When my father was in the hospital dying, he couldn't bear to "bother" the nurse. "The poor soul, she's got three kids at home," he'd say, waving off our pleas to ring the bell in the night and ask for more morphine.

Many of us had so much silence and so many secrets in our families that we adopted a strategy. We learned to hold our breath, present a façade to the world for as long as we possibly could, and when we couldn't hold our breath for one more minute, we withdrew, disappeared, pretended we were someone else. That is not to blame our families; it's to acknowledge that we're adults now and that the survival strategies we developed as children no longer serve us.

At some point we have to say, *I am willing to try things another way. I am willing to face my deepest wounds and do something about them.*

At some point, we have to face the fear, the anger, the anxiety, the part of us that somewhere, sometime, a long, long time ago decided "I will not be hurt again."

CHAPTER TWENTY-TWO

WHILE WE HEAL, WE'RE ALLOWED TO THRIVE

"Pride goeth before a fall," "Geez, I hate a guy who blows his own horn," and "I hate a clingy child" were thoughts I heard frequently as a kid from my parents. People, places, and things can take on a kind of under-earning "energy." We can't save others by depriving ourselves, taking on their guilt, or staying small. People-pleasing and hyper-responsibility can kill. What other people do and how other people live there is their business. But we're "allowed" to thrive.

We're allowed to thrive, and at some point I also had to realize that the shame I felt over the meager portions my mother served to my friends was not the problem of my willing-to-share-everything-she-had mother; the fault was mine. At some point I had to realize that my conflict over the possibility of earning more money than my blue-collar father was not my father's problem: It was mine.

A few years after I got sober, for example, my (now late) father recommended a couple of mutual funds in which to put the nest-egg IRAs with which I left my job as a lawyer. He died a decade later, and for another decade after that, even though I could see one of them had begun to lose money, I couldn't bring myself to even think of asking for help, transferring to another fund, or changing the money in any way. I thought that to change the fund he'd picked out would mean he'd been wrong. I felt changing would have been disloyal.

I finally saw that my father wouldn't have sat around watching the fund lose money; he would've done his homework and changed it. I proceeded truly to honor my father by doing the same thing.

We help poor people not by compulsively staying poor ourselves, but by sharing our material and emotional riches with them. We do our families proud by coming fully awake and fully alive.

CHAPTER TWENTY-THREE

EVEN OUR WOUNDS ARE FROM LOVE

One reason money has loomed so large in my life is that, from childhood, money represented sacrifice, hard work, all that was decent and true. Spending money therefore made me *sad*. I wanted things to stay the way they were! Money represented the way things used to be, either when I was a child, or when I'd earned the money, and I wanted to freeze those moments in time. I wanted to cling to the past, to outwit death.

That impulse, however disordered, came from love: from gratitude, and a desire to keep the connections I'd made at any given time alive. But authentic love calls us to grow up, become responsible, stretch.

CHAPTER TWENTY-FOUR

MAKING THE PEOPLE WE'VE WRONGED WHOLE

The essential, overarching principle of recovery is rigorous honesty. And that means going to the people we've harmed, if any, and offering to make them whole.

Let's not mistake "charm" for honesty, nor weaselhood for charm. If your landlady is pissed because you haven't paid the rent, to appear at her door with flowers because you want to wheedle her into letting you stay isn't "an amends;" it's trying to manipulate a business situation. Charm would be to bring flowers *after getting kicked out*, along with an apology and the back rent.

Love is an action, not an emotion.

CHAPTER TWENTY-FIVE

PRAYER AND MEDITATION

Many of us shut down at the first mention of God, often with good reason.

My own idea of God, such as it is, came about when I got sober. I was so incredibly grateful not to be waking up on the verge of the DTs and stumbling down to Sullivan's Tap to swill rotgut vodka gimlets with washed-up cabdrivers and low-level racetrack touts that almost immediately, I looked around for someone to thank. I didn't want to thank an idea, an abstraction. I wanted to thank a Person.

As the late medieval German mystic Meister Eckhart said, "God is greater than God." We don't have to "believe" in God. We only have to long for connection, meaning, truth, beauty, love. We only have to want to be fully human.

Starting my day with an hour or two of silence has been my practice for years. Carmelite contemplative Ruth Burrows emphasizes that there is no technique to be achieved in prayer, no exalted state to reach:

> Prayer is simply being there: open, exposed inviting God to do all God wants. Prayer is not *our* activity, *our* getting in touch with God, *our* coming to grips with or making ourselves desirable to God. We can do none of those things, nor do we need to, for God is there ready to do everything for us, loving us unconditionally.[3]

Prayer, it came to me one recent morning as I listened to the sparrows, is letting God think for me. And yet my role is active.

ACTIONS

1. Think back to a time in your life when things seemed to be coming together and an event occurred that, in retrospect, caused you to shut down, contract, want to stay small. Write a realistic depiction of what *actually* happened. Include an accurate chronology, a description of the people involved, and details (what you saw, smelled, heard, and felt; what was happening in your body).

2. Think of three pacts you signed with your family at birth, for example, I will be the savior, I will be the scapegoat, I will always shine, I will never shine. Are you still honoring the pacts? If so, do you want to still be honoring them?

3. Set yourself up to win. Before you book a gig, make sure you've slept enough, eaten enough, and given yourself enough time to prepare. After you book a gig, draw up a simple Deal Memo (online samples abound).

4. Make a list of the people you owe money to, owe time to, or owe an apology to for being rude, cryptic, withholding, selfish, or cruel. Run the list and the reasons for owing an amends past a friend whom you trust to be rigorously honest. For instance, you don't owe an amends to all the people with whom you've had one-night stands, especially as your real reason in going to him/her would be to start something up again. Make one amends. See how it feels. Keep going.

5. Many people have been helped by the "Set Aside Prayer": "God, let me set aside everything I think I know about you, myself, other people, and the universe." Try praying that every morning, on your knees, for two weeks. Just try it.

TOOL: THE FIFTEEN-MINUTE RULE
The mind of the person fearful around money is plagued by hyperbole: A crown, an oil leak, a new phone is going to cost "thousands of dollars."

Getting a haircut will take "all day." Getting the car fixed is going to take "a month." Preparing for a trip is going to take "five years." Thus, the simplest decisions are sometimes deferred indefinitely.

Also, I don't know about you, but if I can't do it perfectly, I don't want to do it at all. If I'm not going to get some kind of perverse hit off creating drama where none exists, why bother?

To that end, here's a super handy tool: the fifteen-minute rule. The amount of learning, research, or progress that can occur in just fifteen minutes each day is astounding. Over the course of a month a new habit can be formed. Tasks that have been deferred for years can be completed.

Using the fifteen-minute rule, at the end of three weeks, I'd built a website for my editing business. Many days I worked more than fifteen minutes but I didn't *have* to. Giving myself "permission"—to stop after a certain amount of time; to spend (as opposed to save) a certain amount of money each month—wafted a gentle breeze of sanity through my driven, straight-A psyche.

The fifteen-minute rule is a kind of frame within which to avoid doing things obsessively or compulsively or in a way that veers into self-deprivation or punishment. Set a timer: fifteen minutes and you're off the hook. Fifteen minutes and you feel a hundred times better.

Make a decision to spend fifteen minutes a day for a week on each of the following four activities:

a. Keeping your numbers. If your daily numbers, checkbook, and accounts are up-to-date, use the time to organize your desk, delete old computer files, or freshen up your contacts.

b. Some form of prayer and/or meditation.

c. An outreach call.

d. Marketing.

That's a mere one hour per day. See what you've accomplished and how you feel at the end of the week.

Fifteen minutes—check it out.

STORY: JOSH P.

Josh P., thirty-eight, is an avid reader and gifted photographer.

"I've lived my whole adult life in poverty, chaos, and clutter. Being sober for twelve years in AA has definitely helped me from going completely off the edge, but I still make decisions that are not exactly sane. Five years ago, for example, I married a bipolar woman from the Philippines so she could get a green card. Crazy. We weren't even sleeping together! She went to live with someone else, in fact, and though I've always been an isolater, at that point things got really bad. I'd stupidly given her my passwords and I'd go to the ATM in panic-attack mode to check my account balance, never having any idea whether the last check I wrote had bounced, whether I had enough money for groceries, whether I was going to be able to pay my rent. I was working, if at all, as a free-lance photographer, doing weddings and graduations, making very little money. I never did one thing to market myself, never thought of what I did as a business.

"A friend suggested a twelve-step program for money. At first, I was very resistant. Please! I'm screwed up enough as it is. I already spend half my life in meetings.

"But I had just enough faith that a power greater than myself could help that I went. I sat in the back and didn't talk to anybody for months. I did not 'keep my numbers' or really do anything except sit and soak in what people were saying. Slowly I saw that in one way my whole life had been formed around fear of money, fear that I wasn't good enough or competent enough to make money, fear that I couldn't function in a world that had always seemed alien to me.

"So I kept going. I got a sponsor and worked the steps and I don't know how else to put it: I killed my old self. I was no one for a couple of months. For a couple of months, I had no self. And then a new self was born...

"I eventually got a job as a tour guide, driving a bus to the stars' homes in Hollywood. Ten hours a day, six days a week. I did that for six months. I often wondered whether I'd just found a new way to self-deprive, but I also learned through that job that I had things in me I never knew: discipline, perseverance, the ability to be kind to the tourists on the bus though they were often incredibly annoying and my boss was a weasel.

"I was exhausted the whole time, but my recovery people suggested I do four things for myself for fifteen minutes each day. So for fifteen minutes in the morning I'd meditate. Fifteen minutes on my lunch break I'd go online and do my numbers. Fifteen minutes of my dinner break I'd work on my motorcycle: tuning, polishing. Fifteen minutes before I went to sleep I'd read: not for self-improvement or instruction; just something I wanted to read: a novel, some poetry.

"I ended up paying off every penny of the fourteen grand I had in credit card debt. I had enough left over to live on for a few months and to pay someone to build a website for my photography business. I've changed my passwords. And my wife and I are trying to work things out.

"Hope springs eternal. And in the meantime, I'm also still meditating— fifteen minutes every morning and every night."

PART SIX

DATING OUR DREAMS

CHAPTER TWENTY-SIX

GETTING IN TOUCH WITH OUR INNER LEPER

This is the part of the book that taps most deeply into our vulnerability. It's about all the things we have never allowed ourselves to say: I belong. I'm wanted here. I have value. I am cherished. I deserve the best and I want to give all that I am and have.

Outwardly we can be hyper-conscientious: punctual, self-supporting through our own contributions, soldiering through cancer, divorce, the death of a parent. But inwardly we can be treating our money, our bodies, our lives, our time, like lepers, being afraid to "love" those things for fear they will not love us back.

Everything [animate and inanimate] likes to be loved and tended: our teeth, our wounds, our friends, our food, our plants, our money. So much of my life had been spent ignoring those things. *Wake me up when it's over.* If something was broken, *Pretend it will fix itself.*

It's almost as if we're two people: one who knows we really are unique and precious, and one who cowers and cringes through life feeling deep in our hearts that we're failures: every success a fluke, every gain destined to be immediately lost, every love blue-printed for pain and failure.

The solution is deeper than money, but as an incarnate being I need lovingly to tend my money. Otherwise I'll despise the material world in the wrong way.

British mystic Caryll Houselander, also known as "The Divine Eccentric," suffered nightmarish abandonment in her early years, converted to Catholicism, and ever after had a tender affinity for traumatized children. She wrote:

> There are many people in the world who cultivate a curious state which they call "the spiritual life."… The only time they do not regard as wasted time is the time they can devote to pious exercises:

praying, reading, meditations, and visiting the church.

All the time spent in earning a living, cleaning the home, caring for the children, making and mending clothes, cooking, and all the other manifold duties and responsibilities, is regarded as wasted.

Yet it is really through ordinary human life and the things of every hour of every day that union with God comes about.[4]

"Ordinary human life" includes showing up a lot of places, interacting with a lot of people, and performing a lot of tasks that are not wildly glamorous or exciting. My friend Peter, father of three and magazine editor extraordinaire, once observed:

I don't much subscribe to the idea of following my bliss. I was "following my bliss" all those years when I was out there getting wasted.... I don't especially enjoy going to board meetings at my kids' school but I understand that someone has to do it. I'd rather lie in bed all day reading, but I understand I'm called to do my part. And doing my part makes me feel better, makes me almost—I hesitate to use the word—*happy*.

We're not expected to be more sane, more kind, more solvent, or more recovered than we actually are. But if we want self-esteem, we get to do esteemable acts. Making our beds every morning, keeping our word, honoring our commitments, making it a policy, whenever possible, to return phone calls and answer e-mails: all go toward helping us to value ourselves; toward the building of our "house" on solid rock.

Regard the lilies of the field (Matthew 6:28). And also balance your checkbook, buy a decent laptop, and have your oil changed every three thousand miles.

CHAPTER TWENTY-SEVEN

WHAT DO I REALLY WANT?

I used to hear people talking about "visions" and want to throw up. Visions!? My vision was a day of rest. My vision was an hour without fear. Those are worthy visions, and also I'm coming to see that if I don't have a material vision—a bigger desk, a trip I want to take—I'll "save" indefinitely. I'll never get to the time nor the place when I'm "allowed" to spend. If I don't have a picture of something I'm earning toward, I'm going to continue to hoard my money, no matter how much or how little I make.

Let me take a firm stand here against the dreck we sometimes hear bandied about under cover of "self-care." I once heard a ditzy twenty-something say, "I couldn't pay my rent this month, so I'm just really doing self-care. I got a mani-pedi yesterday and then I got *two* massages." I thought, *Isn't your landlord, who you're ripping off, the one in need of "self-care" here? Shouldn't she be getting a massage while* you look for a job?

Also to be avoided is the magical-thinking notion that *If I call myself a photographer or a pianist or a producer or a "healer"* (you hear way more of this than is fair in Southern California), *that means I am one!*

That is not recovery; that is a different kind of delusion and lie. It does dishonor to the people who actually do write or paint or sculpt or compose, and have devoted their lives to honing their craft.

Here's my beef with visions, or the kind of New-Agey visions you tend to hear swirling around "money" circles these days. I've heard people say, "My vision is to win an Academy Award." I've heard people say, "My vision is to sell a script that gets made into a multimillion dollar picture by the end of the year." I've heard people say "My vision is to be a billion-aire, have two children, one a blond, blue-eyed boy, one an adopted Thai girl, a house in the hills, a husband who adores me, and my own number-one, smash-hit show that I write, produce, and star in."

I seldom hear anyone say, "My vision is to be an *excellent* writer" (or director or executive or whatever); the implication is always "I want to be a *rich* writer." My vision since Day One has been to be an excellent writer. My vision is to leave work that endures.

Well, good for me! Why is that relevant? Because to leave work that endures I need to be as honest with myself as possible. I need to be as free from bondage as possible. As long as I'm in bondage, I'm not writing from my very deepest, most authentic self.

Maybe that's why I like the word *vocation* rather than *vision*:

vo·ca·tion

Noun:

1. A strong feeling of suitability for a particular career or occupation.

2. A person's employment or main occupation, esp. regarded as particularly worthy and requiring great dedication.

CHAPTER TWENTY-EIGHT

DEALING WITH REJECTION

When I was still drinking, I used to go on job interviews and say in so many words: "You do not want to hire me. I mean you really, *really* do not want to hire me." I didn't want that much intimacy. I didn't want people to discover my imperfections.

It's probably safe to assume that potential employers aren't looking at us thinking, *Oh how interesting, I'm poised to hire a wounded, incompetent hobo!* Actually if they're anything like us—and why wouldn't they be?— they're probably thinking mostly about themselves. People wouldn't ask about our services or for an interview if they hadn't noticed we have something of value to offer. To make a big deal out of agonizing about the prospective job when we're lucky anyone's even interested borders on unseemly drama-queenism and self-pity. Suit up, show up, cry alone in the car, and shore up a friend.

Skewed perception will make us invite rejection, interpret neutral events as rejection, and overblow rejection when it actually does occur. In response to my *hemorrhaging* heart, a guy once asked: "Haven't you ever been rejected before?" Granted, he could have been more suave. Granted, he could have been more chivalrous. Later, though, I realized—Well, *haven't* I ever been rejected? In fact, I had known a lot of success. I had been chosen for many things. My magnifying mind made this particular rejection feel gigantic, cataclysmic, life-defining.

We might not be able to control how people react to us, or see us, or feel about us. But we can train ourselves not to be crushed. We can learn not to take it personally—even if it's personal.

CHAPTER TWENTY-NINE

FROM JOB B TO JOB A: DATING OUR DREAMS

Overview/Definition of Job A, Job B

Job A is the dream job. Job B is the job that we may or may not love but that supports us while we seek or do Job A.

Clarity: The Two Lists

I'd grasped back when I was lawyering that "success" consisted in spending as many hours a day as possible doing what I loved. My urge, desire, call to write was so strong I finally reached the point where I knew I *had* to follow it. But if you don't have a call of that kind, here's one idea that might help.

Make two lists. One is "What I Love To Do" and one is "What I'm Good At." You might think these would be the same, but they're not. For example, I love to play the piano but I'm not good at it, or I'm good at bartending but I don't love it.

Then write down the things that appear in both lists, plant a seed, and start praying like mad.

The idea is to see what you're both good at and what you love, and to think not so much about how you could make money but of how the things might combine to produce something entirely unexpected and new.

Why Do We Resist Earning?

I once had a job writing a $400 essay every month for twelve months. The deadline for each essay was six months before publication: December's essay was due in June and so on. I needed money. The essays could, of course, be turned in earlier. I didn't have anything else that needed immediate attention. Yet my strategy was to ration the job out so it lasted the whole year, so $400 would dribble in at a time, so the work wouldn't "run out." One day I realized, *That's a $4,800 job; why not do the whole thing in a few months? And then* look for more work?…

Why are some of us so resistant to earning? For me, a big part of it was that I simply didn't want to interact with people. "Not in a dickish way," as Robert observed of his own clients. "I just didn't much care what they wanted; what they thought; what they needed."

Well, this is the thing of life. You kind of *have* to work up some kind of caring about what "they" want, what they think, what they need. Or else you're going to be spending a lot of time in your room alone eating Top Ramen and watching Netflix.

Common thoughts at Job B workplace, for example, include: *Everyone else is having fun while I have to earn and be responsible. The rest of the world is "in nature" while I'm waiting on tables. "They're" sipping absinthe while I'm doing a spreadsheet.*

In fact, however, while we're drudging away, we're often learning skills that can come in surprisingly handy later on. After the fact, for example, I discovered that my years of lawyering had given me skills that were useful in creative writing: I'd learned to build a coherent argument, issue-spot, and discipline myself to sit in a chair for as long as it took to finish the task at hand.

Getting a Job Physically Doing What We Think We Want to Do

Maybe we haven't yet dared to start doing what we love. Maybe we're trying to figure out what we love. We don't *have* to be moving on to anything. But if we're aware of and troubled by any form of dysfunction around money, we may be willing to at least start dying to our overspending or underearning selves. We're ready to abandon ourselves to God in spite of our fear. The *proof* of abandonment is that we start looking for some kind of work that will allow us to live humanely: either as we work at what we love, or by working Job B as we pursue our passion (Job A).

If you want to be a writer, for example, start looking for a way to support yourself that will allow you a minimum of two hours a day to write. If you want to work in TV, get a job as a personal assistant and give the work everything you have. Show up. Participate. Observe. Be patient. And be honest about how you feel about the work once you're actually doing it.

For us dreamers, reality can come as a harsh surprise. On the other hand, when I started writing, the life was exactly as I'd imagined it, but better. The long hours of silence and solitude; the ability to make my own schedule; the freedom to let my imagination roam felt immediately like the home I'd been looking for all my life—which may be the best guide I know as to whether or not a particular activity is your vocation.

Combining the Two Worlds

There is no shame in any job, done well and with love.

So right-size (take the shame out of) Job B.

Then start approaching Job B the same way you would, or do, Job A—that is, as a way to be of total service to the world. If your job is to hang pictures, pray for the people who are going to be looking at them. Make the holes as if you were making them for your guardian angel.

Catherine de Hueck Doherty (1896–1985) was a Russian émigré and mystic who founded Madonna House, a lay Cathoic community serving the poor. In *Strannik* (a Russian word meaning "pilgrim"), she tells the story of working as a salesclerk in a department store. When the personnel manager learned that Doherty was making the highest commissions, he called her in and asked how it was that she was such a good salesclerk.

> I said, "Well, I don't do anything special. I like selling, but that's not the point. The point is that I made a contract with your company to be on the job eight hours a day. There is my lunch hour, and there are moments when I have to depart from the floor—nature

calls! But I consider all the rest of that time to be yours. I do not consider it as time to chat with the other salesclerks, or to go and powder my nose again and again. I consider a contract to be a moral affair, the moreso because I also made it with God".... A pilgrim knows that he has to walk on this road of obedience to his superiors, whoever they are. I had a moral obligation to spend eight hours a day selling. If I didn't want to sell, I could quit, but I couldn't fritter away the time, for that would be wrong. The pilgrim knows that he walks the road of moral obligation which is, after all, the duty of the moment. My duty was selling...[5]

When we approach our jobs as trusted servants, the world shifts. Opportunities "appear"—possibly because being of service opens our eyes to the opportunities that have been there all along. Ways to combine what we're good at and what we love coalesce. Newfound courage nerves our arm; a sharpened sense of humor helps us to withstand failure, setbacks, and defeat.

There's the gal who took the crap job at Starbucks in order to pay off her debts, ended up loving it, and became regional manager. There's the guy who started selling tube socks at swap meets, moved up to clerking at a record store, and now produces albums. The keys are humility, gratitude, and patience.

ACTIONS

1. Do fifteen minutes of free-form writing on the following: Who would I be if I weren't "poor?" Imagine yourself "rich." What would that look like?

2. What's your vision? What's your vocation? If they're the same, fall to your knees and thank God. If they're not, why not?

3. Set aside fifteen minutes. Using free-form writing, describe your ongoing transformation. Write how you tend to see yourself from within through the lens of your money wound and how you honestly think other people see you from without.

4. If you already know your vocation:
   a. Write what the Job A and Job B are for you.
   b. Make a list of what you love, like, hate about Job B.
   c. Extracting the Job A from Job B:

   Move the love/like elements into the Job A category; see how they're similar. Think about how the job you have now and "hate" is actually teaching you some of the skills you'll need for your dream job that you'll love. Write down five of them. Share them with a friend.

5. If you're trying to figure out what your vocation might be, make "The Two Lists": in one column "What I'm Good At," and in another column, "What I Love." Sit with the two lists for a week or two or three. Look at them each morning. Hold them loosely. Water the seed.

   Now make a third list of the things that, in your mind, make a money-earning enterprise combining what you love to do and what you're good at "impossible": for instance, "I don't know how to keep books, I can't stand to be with people all day, nobody ever makes any money doing that, I'm too old, people will think I'm stupid, I'll fail." Then burn that list. Because that is the voice of Satan.

7. For a week, apply for two jobs a day in your A job field.

8. For a week, do fifteen minutes a day of research into marketing, the jobs available in your field, or ways you could support yourself as you write, make films, compose, paint, garden, or otherwise pursue your A job.

9. For a week, consciously try to treat every person you meet in the course of your workday as Christ. That's right. Try to treat that person, no matter how overbearing, toadying, or annoying, like the Son of Man come to earth. You'll be well on your way to not just dating, but *marrying*, your dream.

TOOL: PRESSURE RELIEF

The disease presses inward, making us ever smaller, angrier, more fragile, and more volatile. One way to relieve the pressure is to get together with a couple of people we trust—one male, one female is best, for a kind of archetypal re-parenting experience—and show them three months' worth of the numbers we've been keeping.

The first time I did this, my people said, "Zero on entertainment?" I replied, "But the ways I entertain myself don't cost anything! I read, I take walks, I play the piano, I knit!" They said, "That is great, but those are all things you do alone. Maybe you'd want to set aside fifty dollars a month and have a night on the town with some friends."

Gentle, in other words. Toward love. Toward community.

I've also heard things from "my people" that at first made me cringe. One guy suggested that I repeat to myself three times a day, "I am a Money Magnet." Personally, I would rather die in the street than say, "I am a Money Magnet" even once. On the other hand, I had to ask myself, would an "affirmation" or two *hurt*? So I said, "I am a Money Magnet" three times a day for two days and I'm not even kidding, a $7,000 job appeared out of nowhere.

No magic here, or rather the "magic" is simply that communing more, fellowshipping more, participating more inevitably helps things shift. I was asking more questions, following more leads, more willing to "look stupid" because I'd finally realized that what was really stupid was continuing to hoard my money and thinking that my life was going to change for the better.

I became more willing to invite others in. I became more willing to try someone else's way.

So here's a radical idea: Find two people, a man and a woman, who are doing this work and who would be willing to sit down for an hour and a half and go over your numbers. Call them.

If one or both say no, think of two more. Call them.

STORY: LISA G.

Lisa G., forty-six, owns a vintage clothing store in the hipster LA neighborhood of Silver Lake.

"I'm an only child who grew up in Manhattan with Hungarian Jewish Holocaust-survivor parents who were all 'Do not trust *anyone*, ever... and especially not God.' I came to LA in my mid-twenties to pursue a career in acting. When after several years that ran its course, I took a retail job in a vintage shop. I ended up working there for three years, searching the whole time for my 'niche.' I actually love vintage, and I loved schmoozing, but where was I going with that? Meanwhile I was constantly in debt, overspending on meals out, clothes here and there, day trips: small amounts that didn't seem like they should add up, but did. I never had any idea how much money I had or how much I spent.

"One day I was discussing my money woes with a friend when she asked, 'Have you ever thought of going to DA?' I'd been sober almost fifteen years, but DA? I thought DA was for people who gambled, or had declared bankruptcy fifty times. 'No,' my friend said, 'it's just about bringing God into your money life.'

"So I started going to meetings with her. The first time I heard the phrase 'vision board' I almost retched, but eventually I started to see the folks there were on to something, even if I couldn't put my finger on what it was. Then my friend turned me on to The Two Lists, which isn't even a program thing but just something that was going around...

"So I wrote down what I loved and what I was good at, and for the first time I realized I'd actually learned a bunch of 'business' skills at my retail job. I knew how to inventory, how to keep books, how to attract and keep customers, how to compile mailing lists. I shared my numbers a couple of times with people I trusted, was willing to take suggestions, continued doing the footwork, and prayed. And it took a couple of years but I went from this kind of desperate *How am I going to make enough money to pay my freakin' rent?* to *How can I...have fun?* Work hard, of course, I didn't mind working—but have fun. Contribute. Participate. *And* make money. I underwent a whole turn from this cramped, mingy, tight-fisted fearful way of being around money to an expansive, roomy, I-can-breathe kind of feel!

"After that, and I know it sounds hokey but it's true, literally in the space of a week things fell into place. A partner appeared, a rental space showed up, I arranged to take the cartloads of vintage I'd collected over the years out of storage in New York and have them shipped here.

"My shop is so much more than a shop. Women come in to try on wedding gowns, women come in to model cocktail dresses for their boyfriends, women come in to drink lattes and kvetch about money, jobs, cars, apartments, their hearts, their men.

"I'm still nuts, and can go into financial fear on a dime, but money is no longer an end in itself with this huge metaphysical weight about my value as a human being. And I'm right in the center of the best, wackiest community in the world."

PART SEVEN

LEAP

CHAPTER THIRTY

WE ALREADY HAVE EVERYTHING WE NEED

Money is good. Money is necessary. Earning a humane living is the very ground of spirituality.

But the real question is: What is the money for? What am I going to do with this resurrected life?

The gifts aren't "out there;" the gifts are inside us. The goal isn't to attract people and money to us; the goal is to *be* us.

We don't want to deprive ourselves, but let's also be clear that we can lead rich, full, absorbing, useful lives without owning a house, a new car, or a closetful of clothes.

To figure out how we want to spend our time is our birthright. To develop our imagination is our sacred responsibility. To continue on the path we know is right for us—not necessarily for anybody else—with very little, if any, encouragement or validation is our primary task.

CHAPTER THIRTY-ONE

WE DON'T NEED TO HOLD OUR GIFTS HOSTAGE

We may not owe anyone money, but we may be withholding our deepest selves. Out of resentment, the desire for a kind of revenge, we may have deprived certain people, and the world, of our talents, time, and gifts.

Authentic spirituality never includes hoarding or scheming or manipulating, and it *never* involves punishing or depriving ourselves or others. To patiently endure hardship when it comes in the natural course of events, or as the unavoidable price/gift of doing what we love is one thing, but to inflict it on ourselves as part of a financial plan always goes toward inertia and death.

Vow-taking, harsh self-discipline, and stiffly-imposed willpower avail us nothing against compulsive self-debting. As with the gifts, the healing isn't "out there"; the healing is inside us.

There will be enough money, enough time, enough love for us. But we get to make the goal giving and sharing with others.

CHAPTER THIRTY-TWO

TO BRING BEAUTY INTO THE WORLD COSTS

Dostoevsky observed, "The world will be saved by beauty." And make no mistake: to bring beauty into the world costs. You can't spend tens of thousands of hours in the solitude required to, say, produce excellent art, and not pay a price. You can't say that big a yes without saying many smaller nos.

Saying that big yes takes tremendous heart, for which we hold our heads high. We no longer advocate for our limitations. Whether we're editing someone's manuscript, or writing a cover letter to submit our own manuscript, or asking for a raise, we no longer think, *Just let me get through this.* We no longer have to scheme how to scrimp or hoard and thereby miss our whole lives.

I would still rather live under a freeway overpass and write the truth, if that's what it came to, than live in a house in the hills and write dreck. I just no longer believe that's what it *must* come to.

CHAPTER THIRTY-THREE

ADOPT THE SPIRITUALITY OF IMPERFECTION

Wanting ourselves to be "better" or more healed than we are can lead to a constant, low-grade hostility against ourselves, the world, and reality itself.

The fact is that for some of us, for whatever reason, a corner of our psyche is simply miswired around money. We can be aware of the miswiring. We can try to take "contrary action." But our miswiring may be one of those things that is painful to us but that doesn't necessarily stand in the way of our usefulness to God and to our fellows.

We are not going to "shape ourselves up," in other words. When the waitperson gestures toward my half-eaten meal and asks, "Do you want to take the rest of this home?" I am never, in this world, going to reply, "No." Nor, probably, should I. I am never going to be able to walk on by a box of free clothes someone's left on the sidewalk without at least peeking.

We are not going to be perfect around money or anything else. We do the best we can, taking into consideration our desires, our limitations, our temperament, and our wounds. Nonetheless, I have come to see that an occasional bromeliad cutting, or a circa-1994 laser printer, or someone else's sparrow green ribbed skirt that they've put out with the trash is probably going to be able to bear the sorrow of being hauled off to the landfill. (If you're a rag-picker type, don't ever read Hans Christian Andersen's "The Christmas Tree.")

Maybe the highest form of spirituality is simply to bear patiently with our brokenness. In the midst of a world of emotional and psychological violence, perhaps we can at least refrain from violence of any kind toward ourselves.

CHAPTER THIRTY-FOUR

AIM FOR THE CHOPPING BLOCK

Deep down, we all have a sense that we were put on earth for something. We have a mission and our hearts yearn to discern what that mission is. Often we come close, but we sense what we've found isn't quite the whole thing or the real thing. Not to fret, because if our hearts are pure, we'll be led to it.

We start to see that everything is a miracle; everything is a sign. So we pay attention to what and who comes through our door, into our mailbox, across our path.

As Annie Dillard says, "Aim for the chopping block. If you aim for the wood, you will have nothing. Aim past the wood, aim through the wood; aim for the chopping block."

Whether we miss doesn't matter. That we aimed for the chopping block, all our lives; with all our heart, mind, soul, and strength, is what matters.

CHAPTER THIRTY-FIVE

LEAP

If we've been following along, healing in community, keeping track of our numbers, we're prepared. We have a safety net. We begin to trust the intuition and hunch. We begin to think, *By God, maybe I could quit my accounting job to write.* Or, *Maybe I could quit my job as a kindergarten teacher to become an accountant.* Or, *Maybe I could plant a garden, make a documentary film, have a baby...*

To work toward what we love, to seek the truth, to serve others, to give all we have—and then receive a hundredfold in return—simply are laws of the universe.

Personally when I quit my job as a lawyer to write I leapt. I didn't know if I was good at it: I leapt anyway. I didn't know if I'd ever make any money: I just leapt.

However much or little we've abandoned ourselves, what other great things might come to pass for us and countless others if we abandoned ourselves even more?

ACTIONS

1. Get quiet and to the best of your ability, get honest. Then go to the deepest part of your heart, to the quietest, purest place inside you, and for fifteen minutes meditate on the most troublesome relationship in your life.

Then do fifteen minutes of free-form writing on the effect the relationship has had on:

a. Your ability to earn.

b. The way you spend your time.

c. The success of your vocation or career.

d. Your other relationships.

2. Take five actions to earn more in the course of doing work that you love. They don't need to be dramatic. If you're a potter, google five pottery sites and see how much people make for hand-thrown mugs, bowls, and tiny wasabi trays. If you've finally figured out that as a writer, composer, or painter, what you have is *a business*, call the bank and ask five questions about opening a business account.

3. List ten of the authors, composers, painters, architects who have paid a price to bring beauty into the world and who have *saved your life*. Give thanks for them. Do ten minutes of free-form writing on the price you've been willing to pay to bring beauty in the world, in spite of your pain, suffering, loneliness, and blocks. Acknowledge yourself for it.

4. Research a vacation. The typical compulsive poverty response to "vacation" is: "Do I *have* to?" No, we don't *have* to. But if we don't realize that our most precious asset is ourselves and that we need to rest *once* in a while, we've veered off into self-deprivation.

So, set aside fifteen minutes every day for a week and just *research* a vacation. Flight, hotels, food, what you want to see, experience, and—maybe even (just a trinket)—buy.

5. Think of something you've been dying to do: play the piano, knit, take photos, cook—but that you don't feel you'd be good at. Spend fifteen minutes researching community college classes, online classes, continuing education classes. You don't even have to sign up—unless you *want* to. Just research.

6. Make a list of twenty-five ways to earn. You're going to say *I don't know even one way to earn.* But you do. You don't know how to walk a dog, wash dishes, clean a house, organize a closet, deliver a pizza?

So make your list. Then sit for a day or two and stare happily out the window.

Then leap.

TOOL: CREATIVE NEGOTIATING

Many people believe, I've learned, that if you write of spirituality, you will and should write for free. Or speak for free. Or read other people's manuscripts, blogs, essays, book proposals and books and give them feedback for free.

So when I started hearing advice like the following, it struck me as revolutionary: "Think of the absolute most money you can imagine making a month—then add a zero. Base how much you charge for your services on that." "Think of absolute highest you think the job is worth and the absolute lowest. Then ask for the absolute highest."

My fear was that I'd ask for what I thought I was worth, the potential client would refuse, and I'd lose the chance to make even the paltry sum they'd offered. This is where I had to be willing to say, "Sorry, _____ is just not in my budget" or "I really can't do it for less than _____" or "How about this? I do it for ___ and you pay door-to-door travel, a $50 meals per diem, lodging, and a professional videographer to do a reel for me that I can use to get more speaking gigs."

Interestingly, I found that "they" will very rarely say no. I found that the way of human commerce is *to negotiate.* I have many "success" stories in this area but I'll offer just one.

I'd agreed to do a talk at a downtown LA locale for a friend of a friend who worked for a cultural organization. "We just love your stuff!" they gushed. "It will be so great; you can invite all your friends."

Months passed and then one morning I thought, *Why am I doing this for free?* The other guy who was doing the talk was coming from Ireland: you can be sure he was getting paid. So I overcame the fear that at this late date to ask to be paid would be churlish and e-mailed my friend and said, "I see I've neglected to ask what kind of stipend you're planning on paying!" So he e-mailed back and said, "We were thinking $300, is that OK?" I wrote back, "Come now, I'm trying to make a living! I was thinking $1,000—even my nonprofit fee would be $750." And damned if the guy, bless his heart, didn't shoot back, "We're happy to pay you the $1,000."

And if they're not happy, here's what you get to realize: *They can't afford me.*

In that vein, how long has it been since you asked for a raise, raised your fees, and/or researched the going rates for your profession?

Just wondering.

STORY: DONALD N.

Donald N., forty-eight, is a health care advocate, massage therapist, soup kitchen volunteer, and gardener.

"I had a lifelong habit of earning only the bare minimum. In my mind in order to earn decent money I'd have to sacrifice my freedom. I'd have to do something I really didn't like, or get a job where I worked endless hours and therefore couldn't pursue my art and community service.

"My way worked for a long time. I didn't mind driving a little beat-up car, or living in a rented room, or only taking a vacation if I could camp or sleep on someone's sofa. I lived for years at the LA Catholic Worker (a lay community that runs a Skid Row soup kitchen and witnesses for social justice issues). We got a fifteen-dollars-a-week stipend and I had a little house-painting job on the side and that was all I needed! My shelter and food and access to a vehicle and entertainment needs, 'cause there were so many people around, were taken care of.

"When I left the Catholic Worker, I got a job for a nonprofit doing healthcare advocacy. I worked my way up so I was making about $26,000 a year.

"But then I got married. And at that point, it was no longer just about me; it was about us. Being a couple, maintaining a house. Ellen is a teacher at the top of her pay grade, and makes $70,000 or so a year. She was making a lot more than me—that was OK; I contributed to the household in ways other than money—but I started to skimp on myself because any money I had was going toward our common stuff. And I was wanting a little more. My feet started hurting, for example, because I was always wearing used or worn-out shoes. There's a reason all the guys on Skid Row have lousy feet: They don't have adequate shoes.

"I was also unhappy with my situation at work. I didn't feel I was being adequately paid for the expertise I'd brought to the job and developed there. In twelve years, my hourly pay had increased only three dollars.

"So I reached a point where a breakthrough had to come. I finally worked up the courage to quit. For a few months I did odd jobs, picking up trash, whatever I could. Then one of my crowns broke, which was going to cost a lot of money. And one morning I was going to go pick up some items for my friend Ampora, who's mentally disabled, and whose SSI money I oversee. I didn't want to go to the grocery store because that'd be too expensive so I went to the 99-Cents Only Store. I was so preoccupied that I forgot to feed the meter and when I came out I had a $60 ticket. I didn't even beat myself up. I was totally cool with it because

I knew right away that parking ticket was my little lesson; a window onto a new way.

"Just before this, my old job had asked if I'd come back as a consultant. I'd said, 'Sure, let's talk,' but I was so afraid of underselling myself that my plan had been to go in with an attitude of *This is what I'm worth: take it or leave it.* Sitting in my car outside the 99, though, I realized, *They need me. I need the job. There's no reason on earth why it shouldn't work out.* And somehow I started thinking, Why not go in with the attitude of *How can we both walk away happy here? How can we* both *get what we want and need?* Let's not have winner/loser, let's have both/and.

"So I wrote an e-mail and I was very specific about what I wanted to do: my title, my hours, my pay, the scope of the work. We met again, and within an hour we'd worked out a gig where I work only two (ten-hour) days a week, doing the employee training that's my strong suit, and where I'm making three times the money per hour I made as a full-time employee.

"That was a huge breakthrough for me. And I'll end with this. Shortly afterward, someone gave me an abandoned beehive. I set it up in the backyard with a concoction of lemon grass oil that, long shot, was supposed to attract the bees.

"A few weeks later I was inside and I heard what sounded like a cyclone. I went outside and the sky was buzzing. A huge swarm of bees had come! Whether going through this process had created the space or whether I had new eyes to see, right away I knew the bees were a 'sign.'

"Put the 'energy' out there; the money comes."

THE NUMBERS DON'T LIE

During the course of this work, I was lucky enough to have a brilliant spiritual mentor, an ordinary guy like you or me who mirrored back the truth to me in the *most* loving way. He listened to my resentments, my fears, my secrets around emotions and money. He helped me see that beneath my money "issues" were grandiosity, impatience, hostility, sloth, and pride.

He encouraged me to take all kinds of actions to which I was initially resistant. I built a website for my editing business. I took a teaching job. I started asking for way more than I thought I'd be given for speaking gigs. I started saying yes to people, places, and things I would have said no to before.

I started earning more, spending more, and giving away more: more time, more love, more money. I underwent a genuine spiritual awakening. Everything that had made sense to me before—to earn and to spend as little as possible in favor of spending the maximum amount of time working—now seemed self-defeating and insane. I'd constructed my own little business empire of one. I'd professed to believe that we are all part of one Mystical Body, but I hadn't been able to totally live that out.

The numbers tell only part of the story. As Jesus said to the paralytic, "Which is easier, to say, 'Your sins are forgiven,' or to say, 'Rise and walk?'" (Matthew 9:5). The real deal is the inner healing; the inner freedom. But just to show he was who he said he was, Jesus helped the guy to get up off his mat. To walk. To go home.

And just to show these actions work, here are three months' worth of my own numbers pre-recovery and the same three months a year later.

Pre-Recovery

MARCH:

In: 502.22

Out: 2,508.78

-2,006.56

APRIL:

In: 1,065.16

Out: 3,837.51

-2,772.36

MAY:

In 2,600.42

Out: 2,008.35

+592.07

Average for three months:

In: 679.16

Out: 2,784.88

-2,105.72

• • • • • •

Monthly breakdown by category:

MARCH:

In:

Blog donation: 172.22

Books: 30

Magazine editing: 300

Out:

Spirituality: 67.40

Shelter: 806.54

Food: 206.66

Transportation: 100.21

Clothing: 324.87

Personal Care: 99.31

Health Care: 85.00 (I have no

health insurance, obviously.)

Entertainment: 0

Education: 0

Vacations: 0 (Though I housesat the whole month at a friend's nice place in Palm Springs.)

My Business: 812.25

Gifts: 6.54

Investments: 0 (Though I changed over some non-returning mutual funds.)

Taxes: 0

Debt Repayment: 0 (I have no debt: had one credit card I paid in full each month for years: have cut it up and switched to debit card.)

APRIL:

In:

Magazine writing: 300

Royalties: 179.35

Editing: 51.90

Gift: 240

Blog donation: 293.90

Out:

Spirituality: 120.09

Shelter: 831.45

Food: 267.13

Transportation: 1,449.32

Clothing: 42.72

Personal Care: 79.03

Health Care: 511.86

Entertainment: 10

Education: 0

Vacations: 0

My Business: 106.86

Gifts: 0

Investments: 0

Taxes: 481.45

Debt Repayment: N/A

MAY:

In:

Magazine writing: 1,750

Editing: 500

Blog donation: 96.80

Royalties: 103.62

Gift: 150

Out:

Spirituality: 100.15

Shelter: 926.53

Food: 201.97

Transportation: 194.33

Clothing: 6.81

Personal Care: 50.11

Health Care: 65.96

Entertainment: 0

Education: 0

Vacations: 0

My Business: 462.49

Gifts: 0

Investments: 0

Taxes: 0

Debt Repayment: N/A

Post-Recovery

MARCH:

In: 4,625.51

Out: 2,386.36

+2,239.15

APRIL:

In: 1,996.28

Out: 2,914.24

-917.96

MAY:

In: 5,346.21

Out: 5,819.07

-472.86

Average for three months:

In: 3,989.33

Out: 3,706.56

+282.77

• • • • • •

Monthly breakdown by category:

MARCH:

In:

Speaking: 3,000

Teaching: 703.25

Magazine writing: 400

Books: 242.99

Royalties: 62.67

Blog donation: 216.60

Out:

Spirituality: 238.00

Shelter: 800.00

Food: 273.28

Transportation: 143.51

Clothing: 478.12

Personal Care: 97.01

Health Care: 0

Entertainment: 60.00

Education: 0

Vacations: 0

Personal Business: 0

My Business: 273.96

Gifts: 22.48

Investments: 0

Taxes: 0

Debt Repayment: N/A

APRIL:

In:

Magazine writing: 350

Speaking: 750

Teaching: 394.96

Books: 51

Editing: 400

Royalties: 50.32

Out:

Spirituality: 248.00

Shelter: 814.42

Food: 298.24

Trans.: 862.57

Clothing: 0

Personal Care: 87.02

Health Care: 241.56

Entertainment: 60.00

Education: 0

Vacations: 0

My Business: 186.26

Gifts: 60.15

Investments: 0

Taxes: 116.00

Debt Repayment: N/A

MAY:

In:

Speaking: 3,250

Royalties: 108.41

Blog donation: 95.80

Books: 92.00

Magazine writing: 1,500

Editing: 300

Out:

Spirituality: 52.78

Shelter: 829.39

Food: 260.70

Transportation: 122.07

Clothing: 538.33

Personal Care: 49.22

Health Care: 0

Entertainment: 4.00

Education: 0

Vacations: 0

My Business: 2,056.11 (I bought 200 of my own books at cost which I will sell for $9 profit per.)

Gifts: 16.47

Investments: 0

Taxes: 1,890

Debt Repayment: N/A

MONEY IS A MEANS, NOT THE END

Trusting that money will continue to flow in has allowed me better to experience money exactly how it should be experienced: as an asset, a gift, a tangible form of abundance that I can spend on what I need and, even better, give away. Five hundred bucks to the Catholic schools in LA, a few hundred bucks to a friend who had an apartment fire, a hundred dollars here and there to feed the poor and shelter the homeless, an envelope for the funeral of a nephew in El Salvador. More money to church, more money to help the people in prison, more money to the many panhandlers I run into on my daily walks around LA.

To say more would ruin it; the best kind of giving is done in secret. And the best kind of giving is also not of money, but of heart.

When all is said and done, I live pretty much as I have for decades. I've found the best way to ensure that I enjoy food is always to be a tiny bit hungry. The best way to enjoy a new jacket is to wear the old jacket for several years first.

But more and more, my actions are based on love, not fear. It's almost as if I had to learn that I *could* make money in order to begin to healthily detach from money.

Recently my friend Tensie, who told her story at the beginning of the book, called. As usual, our discussion was intense. We talked about our families and friends, our prayer life, the birdsong we both love. Then she said, "You know, Heather, I've been thinking. And I really think one of the things we're called to do for each other is to be with each other as we die. I don't know how you'd feel but I would really like to offer that to you. It would be a great honor and a privilege, if it comes down to that, to do whatever I can, to be by your side, to help you through."

Besides giving birth, is there a greater gift one person could offer another? It may not have been until that moment that I realized how deeply afraid I had been of dying alone.

To know that even one person of such self-emptying servanthood exists on this earth—now that is wealth. That is the Kingdom of God. That is surely part of what Christ meant in the Sermon on the Mount when he said "Blessed are the poor in spirit."

. . .

Bill Cunningham, the subject of the 2010 documentary *Bill Cunningham New York*,[6] is a fashion photographer who has a very different life and a very different vocation than my friends from the Catholic Worker. Yet he cultivates his own kind of voluntary poverty, and his story thus seems a perfect coda to a book about freedom, love, truth, and above all, beauty.

For years, Cunningham has maintained two spreads in *The New York Times*. "Evening Hours" covers the social, philanthropic, and political world of New York's high society. "On the Street" is an "attempt to tease out trends in terms of the reality of how people dress," observes Harold Koda, curator of the Costume Institute of the Metropolitan Museum of Art. "I really feel he does address the whole spectrum of what we are as New Yorkers and I believe he's the only one who does it."

Cunningham, now eighty-three, rides around Manhattan on an old (donated) Schwinn (his twenty-ninth; the previous twenty-eight were stolen). He gets his film developed at a mom-and-pop convenience store called Photo King, describing himself over the phone to the clerk as "the guy who comes in on a bike." He sleeps in a cot in the same tiny studio above Carnegie Hall where he's lived for decades. The bathroom is down the hall. There are no cooking facilities. He hangs his few clothes off the handles of metal filing cabinets, and come laundry day, carries the bundle on his handlebars to the local Fluff and Fold.

He loves color, cut, the male and female form. He cares nothing for celebrity; he cares profoundly, almost religiously, for clothes, and for the people who wear them.

He also has a patrician Boston accent, the kind of old-school class that forbids self-pity or self-promotion, and his own brand of style—a worn-backwards newsboy's cap, a blue sweater tied over his shoulders. Tall, ascetically lanky, and brisk without being rude, his chief characteristic is a compelling, exuberant joy. "Child," he calls a fifty-year-old woman. "You kids," is his term of affection for the NYT staff with whom he works.

"He's incredibly kind," notes Annette de la Renta, trustee at the Met. "I don't think we've ever seen a cruel picture done by Bill."

Women's Wear Daily, where he was employed in the late '70s, once used his photos in a mean-spirited way, ridiculing the women he'd photographed. Devastated, he quit.

Annie Flanders, founding editor of *Details*, gave Bill 100-page spreads back in the early '80s—for which he refused to be paid. Nor would he take a check from Condé Nast when they took over in 1989.

"If you don't take money, they can't tell you what to do, kid," he chortles. "That's the key to the whole thing. *Don't touch money!*"

Does he refuse money from the *New York Times*? you start to think. Does he give it all away? Bill doesn't say.

By night he photographs celebs and the Brooke Astor set; day in, day out, he himself wears the same kind of sturdy blue smock worn by Parisian street-sweepers.

"Damn you, New Yorkers. You're all so extravagant and wasteful," he teases, repairing a cheap plastic poncho with duct tape before he sets out in the rain again with his camera. "There, we're back in business. I think this embarrasses everyone. But it doesn't embarrass me!"

At the Stage Star Deli, he chows down an English-muffin with sausage and egg. "They make the best sandwich," he crows. "And coffee, three dollars. The cheaper, the better."

Through cold, rain, and snow; by day, by night; he's out there on his bicycle, traversing and trolling Manhattan. "He's like a war photographer," notes Kim Hastreiter, co-editor-in-chief of *Paper Magazine*. "He'll do anything for the shot."

Themes emerge for his "On the Street" column: Shirt Tails and Leggings, Racing Stripes, Polka Dots, Fanny Packs, Baggy Pants, The Denim Dress. "I don't decide anything," Bill avers. "I let the street speak to me. In order for the street to speak to you, you have to stay out there and see what it is. There's no shortcuts, believe me."

Threatened with eviction from his studio, and offered a new, snazzy apartment, he frets, "Who the hell wants a kitchen and a bathroom? Just more room to clean."

When a realtor brings him by a prospective upgrade and shows him the closet, he says, "Well, it would be nice if I had clothes to hang there." "But it's beautiful," she insists, "with the whole wall of windows, and the windowed kitchen facing the park." "That's an embarrassment, isn't it?" he responds.

Some think fashion is frivolous. For Bill, "It's the armor to survive the reality of everyday life. I don't think you could do away with it. It would be like doing away with civilization."

He knows many of the club kids, the drag queens, the rappers by name. "The best fashion show is definitely on the street. Always has been. Always will be. It's never occurred to me that I'm just waiting. It's always the hope that you'll see some marvelous exotic bird-of-paradise."

But while he's in the world, he's not of it. He takes his shots. He pedals off into the night. He keeps his private life, thoughts, and the impetus behind his prodigious drive—his mission—to himself.

"I think (the work) has to be done discreetly, quietly. Invisible to the world."

In Paris for the *haute couture* shows, he reluctantly accepts an award from the French Minister of Culture making him an Officer in the Order of Arts and Letters.

"I don't work," he tells the audience with a boyish grin. "I only know how to have fun every day.... It's as true now as it ever was: He who seeks beauty [choking up] will find it!"

"I'm guessing he may come from wealth," says Annie Flanders, the founding editor of *Details*. "Only people who come from wealth can live the way he does. But I've never actually discussed it with him."

"Just working-class people," Bill describes his family. "Just marvelous normal hard-working people. Catholic people."

Near the end of the film, the interviewer asks, "Have you ever had a romantic relationship?"

"Are you asking if I'm gay?" he cackles. "Well, that's probably why the family wanted to keep me out of the fashion world. They wouldn't speak of such a thing. But no, I haven't.... It never occurred to me. There was no time. I was working night and day.... In my family, such things were never discussed. So it wasn't even in my head or my mind. I wouldn't have known a thing about it. So they needn't have worried...I've enjoyed (my work) so much that it didn't.... But hey, listen, I am human...You do have, uh, body urges or whatever, but, uh, you control it as best you can."

"I know that you go to church every Sunday."

"Oh, yeah."

"And does religion.... Is that an important component of your life?"

Here, Bill, overcome, bows his head and for several moments, is unable to speak.

Finally, he gathers himself. "Yeah, I think it's a good guidance in your life.... It's something I need and...it's part of your upbringing....

Whatever it is, everyone.... You do whatever you do the best you can work things out, but yeah. I find it very important. Yeah. For whatever reason.... As a kid...I went to church and all I did was look at women's hats.... But later, when you mature, (you go) for different reasons."

Here is a man who, at the day of judgment, is going to be able to give the best possible account of himself. He didn't waste his time. He wasn't against anything. He wasn't trying to prove anything. He wasn't judging anyone. He was experiencing existence to the absolute hilt, every second.

I thought: *I hope this man lives forever!*

But of course—he already has.

NOTES

1. Richard Rohr, *Breathing Underwater: Spirituality and the Twelve Steps* (Cincinnati: Franciscan Media, 2011), xxi.
2. Rohr, 31.
3. Ruth Burrows, *Essence of Prayer* (Costa Mesa, CA: Paulist, 2006), 28.
4. Caryll Houselander, *The Reed of God* (Allen, TX: Christian Classics, 2006), 5.
5. Catherine Doherty, *Strannik: The Call to the Pilgrimage of the Heart* (Combermere, ON: Madonna House, 2000), 57.
6. *Bill Cunningham New York* (Zeitgeist Films, 2010), a documentary directed by Richard Press, is widely available on DVD and digital media.